Teach Your Expertise

How to Grow a Business and Become a Success by Creating an Online Class or Program ©2020

Compiled by Alina Vincent

Teach Your Expertise

How to Grow a Business and Become a Success by Creating an Online Class or Program

© 2020 By Alina Vincent

This book may be purchased for educational, business, or sales promotional use. For more information, or to order additional copies of this book, email Alina at Book@BusinessSuccessEdge.com.

All information written in this book is of relevant content and written solely for motivation and direction. No financial guarantees. All information is considered valid and factual to the writers' knowledge. The authors are not associated or affiliated with any company or brand mentioned in the book, and therefore do not purposefully advertise nor receive payment for doing so.

The authors and publisher do not assume and hereby disclaim any liability to any party for any loss, damage, or disruption caused by errors or omissions.

BusinessSuccessEdge.com

ISBN 978-1-7354408-0-4

Library of Congress Control Number: 2020944699

BONUS GIFTS

This book comes with free gifts, exercises, and resources from each of the contributing authors.

You can access all of them on the bonus Resources Page:

TeachYourExpertiseBook.com/gifts

Contents

Dedicated to all Rising Stars who are passionate about sharing their gifts, wisdom, and expertise and serving the world through the power of online programs.

Introduction
The Power of Online Programs:
How to Use Your Experience to Grow Your Business
by Alina Vincent

If you'd asked me just 10 years ago if I saw myself as an entrepreneur, I would have laughed in your face.

And yet, now I could not imagine my life any other way; leading a business that supports thousands of clients while creating a positive impact on their lives and businesses, and running a million-dollar business simply by sharing my knowledge and expertise.

The biggest secret to my success: discovering and embracing the power of online programs.

Online programs provide entrepreneurs with a powerful method for teaching their expertise to the people who need them the most, while growing their business, impact and income.

That's what this book is all about.

On these pages, I'll share with you my journey from struggling to find myself and recognize my own expertise to creating a step-by-step formula for creating profitable online programs. You'll also read success stories and lessons learned from my clients in different stages of business who have used this proven approach for growing their businesses.

But … I'm getting ahead of myself …

Growing up, I had no ambition or desire to start my own business. The thought never even crossed my mind (I was raised in a family of several generations of teachers and college professors struggling to survive on barely middle-class salaries).

The only thing I knew for sure? Teaching was in my blood. As soon as I learned something (and I *loved* learning), I had to share it. As soon as I discovered a simpler way to do something, I wanted others to benefit from what I'd just learned. I just *had* to share what I knew and experienced with others.

"Learn, do, teach" became my motto for life.

So, it probably comes as no surprise that after I graduated from high school, I went straight to college and then to graduate school. For the first 16 years of my adulthood and career, I earned degrees and chased tenure. I spent years studying and teaching at a university where I tried on different careers: life-long student, teaching assistant, lecturer, instructional designer.

A critical component of my job as an instructional designer was to revolutionize the way our university offered classes: we designed educational models that combined traditional in-class teaching with online teaching, or went to online teaching all together (it's pretty commonplace now, but at the time, it was truly groundbreaking).

I encountered many professors who worried that an online educational model (or even a hybrid model) wouldn't replicate the in-person teaching model effectively.

They truly struggled with the idea. They thought it wouldn't work. They were so used to working and interacting in-person that they counted on the online model failing.

But guess what happened?

Invariably, every single professor I worked with said he or she was actually making a **_greater impact_ on their students _online_**!

The courses we created together were more interactive, more powerful, and more personal for them and for their students. More conversations and connections took place online, along with deeper engagement and bigger breakthroughs.

I'm telling you this because I know that changing the way you currently do business can feel unnerving. You may wonder whether you'll be able to share your expertise in the same way if you're not face-to-face with your clients or customers.

You _can_. We'll go into this topic more in the next chapter, but for now, suffice it to say that changing (or challenging) the way you do business can actually be a blessing; you'll likely see your clients or customers achieve even bigger breakthroughs!

As I saw the professors at my university realize the power of going online, I began to sense that there was more for me. I yearned for more creative freedom around what I could explore and teach. I no longer wanted to be held down by the constrains of a job and limitations on what I could create. I knew I could impact more people.

And I definitely knew that I could do more, be more … and earn more. At the time, my annual salary was $40,000 and wasn't set to increase due to recession and statewide salary freezes. People were losing their jobs left and right, and many of my university colleagues got laid off.

Amidst all of that, I made a crazy decision to leave my secure, stable job at the university.

I followed the advice so many people do when they start a business: I turned my passion into a business. Since photography had been my hobby since I was 10, I opened a photography studio.

And I (very mistakenly) thought that if I was good at taking pictures, my business would just grow naturally.

Talk about culture shock!

In my 20s, I'd come to the United States from Uzbekistan (one of the republics of the former Soviet Union), and even that was less of a shock than going from the academic world into the world of entrepreneurship.

As a business owner, I quickly discovered being good at something wasn't enough; having skills and experience wasn't enough; and simply wanting to help and serve people wasn't enough. I had zero marketing skills, I felt completely invisible, I wasn't getting clients, and I wasn't making money.

I had to learn how to market myself, how to build my business the right way, and how to promote and position my offers. I hired a coach, joined a mastermind, and focused on studying marketing (instead of learning cool new photography skills as I thought I would).

It paid off big time.

I grew my photography business from zero to more than six figures in the first 18 months (which was almost unheard of in our industry of "starving artists"). I did it primarily by figuring out how to attract clients from Facebook organically (pay attention here—it will become important in just a bit).

My business was growing, my name was getting out there, and on the surface, everything seemed great.

Even so, I realized that while my business looked really successful from the outside, I was still trading hours for dollars. Instead of creating a business that would give me freedom and flexibility, I had created another j-o-b. And even though it was paying more and I enjoyed more creativity, I was tied to my business because I was providing one-on-one services that depended on me working and being there **all the time**.

As soon as I put down my camera, I stopped making money. If I got sick or wanted to take a vacation, I stopped earning.

I was already charging more for my work than anyone in our area, so if I wanted to grow (earn more money), I had to double the hours I was working (and I already worked seven days a week).

That's when I had a "lightbulb" moment: I'd built a successful business that wasn't scalable and didn't allow me to leverage my time and my efforts.

I knew I had to shift my direction. I began to explore different business models that would allow me to escape the time-for-money trap.

Although I loved photography, I was also getting more comfortable helping other business owners with their marketing. A coach I was working with at the time helped me realize that I was already coaching my photography clients without realizing it, because I was always happy to share what I knew.

He said:

"You know when you're taking marketing headshots for entrepreneurs and asking them what their niche is, who their clients are, who they want to attract, and helping them get clarity on who they are and what they do before you take their pictures? You don't even realize that you've been coaching your clients for years."

He was right.

So I made a decision to let go of my photography studio and start a new coaching business to help entrepreneurs get more visibility and clients online in my new role as a business and technology strategist.

And for the first four months, I struggled. Really struggled. And I couldn't understand why.

I already had the experience of building a six-figure business. I already had the experience of marketing my offers and enrolling clients. I was doing all the right things … participating in a mastermind to get new ideas, attending networking events, setting up discovery sessions with potential clients, posting about my offers, etc. … so *why* could I not get a single client?

That's right: in the first four months, I was turned down by *every single* potential client.

Even though I hated the idea of working for someone again, I reached a point of desperation. I dusted of my resumé and started applying for jobs, because we simply could not make ends meet.

And that's when I realized two *huge* mistakes I had made with my new business (I hope you are taking notes).

The first mistake was that when I started my new coaching business, I completely disregarded all of my past experiences—all of them.

In my mind, I was starting out with a blank slate.

It kind of makes sense, right? How would my degree in engineering help me be a better coach? How did my ability to take great pictures position me as an expert in marketing?

I wasn't writing a new chapter in an existing book (although, I should have been!). I threw away the old book and started a new one, from scratch.

So, it's no wonder that I was approaching every new client with the subconscious mindset that I was "brand new" in this business, and had no credibility or experience. No wonder they all said, "No."

Lucky for you, you can skip learning this lesson the hard way, and take it from me right now:

When you're starting any new venture, business, or direction, you must embrace and leverage every experience, every bit of expertise, every lesson, and every part of the journey that brought you to where you are right now.

Once I realized this, everything clicked into place.

Now I could look at every aspect of what made me unique and qualified to do the work I wanted to do.

I saw that my teaching experience made me good at explaining things to people. My degrees in computer science and engineering helped me organize information in clear, step-by-step instructions. My photography business helped me unleash my creative side and out-of-the box thinking. My time working as an instructional designer gave me experience and expertise in creating online programs.

And that's when I had another "facepalm" moment.

I realized I was making another big mistake.

Even though I wanted to create a more leveraged and scalable business I could easily grow, I wasn't actually doing it. I was once again going after one-on-one clients.

It felt more familiar and, more importantly, I simply couldn't figure out what I could offer to groups of my potential clients based on my limited "official" coaching experience.

Once I had the realization that I should be looking at incorporating *all* of my past experiences into my offers, I immediately got several ideas for online programs I could create based on my existing skills and knowledge.

In the next chapter, I'll share how you can get started with choosing the right idea for your program—one that will not only empower you to leverage your time and expertise by serving your people in a one-to-many model, but could also provide a practical solution to hundreds (if not thousands) of your ideal clients.

I based my first online program on a question I was getting from a lot of entrepreneurs who followed my success in my photography business: "How do you get so many clients from Facebook without using Facebook ads?"

I decided to teach my expertise in this area and share exactly what I do on Facebook to get clients. I called my program Facebook Traffic Explosion, and I offered it in a 21-day challenge format. I sold it for a whopping $57, and it was the sweetest payday I've ever had.

After struggling and not being able to get a single client for months, 47 people enrolled in my program seemingly overnight! Almost four dozen people said, "Yes" and wanted to learn from me. I could already see the power of offering online programs and teaching what came easy to me to grow my business.

Little did I know, that was just the beginning.

Once people started to go through the program and get results, magic happened.

Word spread, and soon, I was known as Alina, *"the lady who created that Facebook program that works."* I was getting recommendations and referrals from my participants. "Big name" coaches and speakers in my industry asked me to speak at their events and wanted to add my program to their list.

Several of the business owners who completed my program reached out to me and wanted to continue working with me privately. I didn't even have to have enrollment conversations with them—they knew they wanted to hire me and did so on the spot!

I went from being a nobody to being a trusted expert, all because I'd created and packaged my step-by-step process into an online program and people were getting results.

Fast forward just three months, and I offered my program again (this time at $297). It resulted in a $20,000 month! I made more in one month than I was getting paid for a half a year of teaching at the university.

Just three months after that, I was invited to speak onstage at a live event, and after one 90-minute presentation, I sold $28,000 worth of my program …

This was working!

I updated and upleveled my existing program, increased my prices and created a couple more programs.

Less than two years after I started this business, it was worth a quarter-of-a-million dollars. Four years later, my business was generating more than a million dollars.

Let that sink in for a minute.

Pretty incredible, right?

The impact my online programs have had on my business and my clients has been amazing.

But even better is the impact online programs have had on my family life. I enjoy incredible support from my entire family (my husband and our two daughters). This program-based online business allows us to travel, explore the world, spend time together, and do what matters most.

And these results are *reproducible*, even if you don't yet see how it could apply to you and your business.

You might be asking yourself:

Can I really do this?

Does it apply to my industry?

Do I know enough to teach others?

How do I come up with the right idea for the program?

Will anyone buy from me?

I get it. When you're standing behind that starting gate, the idea of creating and selling a program may feel like a massive undertaking.

We'll dive into answering these questions (and many more) in the following chapter.

Right now, you're standing on the edge of an amazing opportunity, and I'm so glad you're here.

I, along with all the entrepreneurs in this book, want you to know that creating an online program that powers your business success—in terms of your profitability and freedom—is possible! And we want to make it easier for you. That's why, in each chapter, the contributors share their advice for creating an online program. Plus, as a bonus, each has also offered a special gift around his or her specific expertise.

You'll find those gifts on the Resource Page, here:

TeachYourExpertiseBook.com/gifts

Chapter 1
Start Here: Your Roadmap to Creating and Launching Your First Online Program
by Alina Vincent

You're here! You're standing on the edge of something great … an opportunity to *finally* make your business work … to use it to truly help people *and* to create the freedom for which you work so hard.

First of all, I'm so excited for you! By reading this book, you're taking the first steps toward turning that dream into reality.

Second, I know from experience how overwhelming it can be to start any new venture. I hope this chapter answers some of your biggest questions and moves you from the thinking-about-it phase into action … because *that's* where the magic happens.

Here, I'll share with you my definition of an online program, address some common questions and concerns, and the exact process I use and teach to my students, to design a powerful program that meets the needs of your clients—and makes your business **grow**. This process may look a bit different than what you're expecting, but it's effective.

It has worked for me, over and over, and it has worked for hundreds of my clients. We have followed it to success and freedom, and you can, too.

Let's make sure we are on the same page …

17

First off, what *is* an online program?

An online program (or a course) is a digital training that is delivered via the Internet and packaged in a way that's easily accessible from anywhere in the world. Online programs are designed to lead people through a series of steps to produce specific results or master a new skill.

Your online program is a digital package that contains your knowledge, expertise, and experience on a specific topic. By creating an online program, you're making your unique system or solution available to hundreds (or even thousands) of people who need it.

As you saw in the last chapter, online programs empower business owners to shift away from a one-on-one time-for-money model, to a one-to-many leveraged model with incalculable potential for making positive impact and profit.

A proven program that produces results can easily position you as the go-to expert in your field, create opportunities for passive income, and provide a foundational launching point for other elements of your business (high-ticket offers, coaching packages, done-for-you services, physical products, events, masterminds, apps, software, and more).

Online programs utilize a variety of delivery methods: some offer online modules with videos and transcripts, while others provide written lessons with workbooks. Some are done live with live interaction, coaching, and feedback, while others are delivered as a home-study program that can be consumed at your own pace.

So is an online program the same as group coaching?

Great question!

Because online programs often include coaching calls, many entrepreneurs mistakenly think that they've created an online program when in fact, what they are offering is group coaching.

While both allow you to leverage your time and utilize the one-to-many model, creating a program produces *a leveraged digital asset you can use over and over* (without any additional input from you).

On the other hand, the pure group coaching model relies heavily on your presence and expertise, which you share live and "in the moment" in response to the immediate needs and questions of your group, without following a specific step-by-step content plan.

The main difference between an online program and group coaching is in answering this question: "If you completely remove yourself from the process of delivering the program, will your participants still get the results or transformation that you've promised?" If your answer is yes, you have an online program.

Here is another way to look at it: compare publishing a book to telling a powerful story. Both can be very effective in creating transformation. However, once your book is written, it lives outside of you and can transform the lives of your readers even if they never have a single interaction with you. When it comes to telling a story live, you must tell it again and again in order to continue having an impact.

So, if your program relies primarily on you delivering content or coaching, teaching, and mentoring live, you have a group coaching program, where you are the linchpin holding everything together.

If, however, you've designed your training in a way that allows your participants to get results even if you are not around to actively contribute to their learning, congratulations! You've succeeded in creating an online program.

Do you need to be an established expert before you can create a program?

So many entrepreneurs believe they need to be working in their business for years before they can create a program, or that they need to be recognized (or "verified") experts. Nothing is further from the truth.

You *are* enough.

You don't need another degree or training. You don't need another certification. You don't need someone's permission. You don't need 10 more years of experience.

You already have a skill, a gift, a talent, an experience, knowledge, and expertise you can package into an online program and sell. I guarantee it.

Once you understand that and begin to look at your entire life as a source for discovering and teaching your expertise, you'll be unstoppable.

Your message, your ability to help people, is already within you. Every success, every failure, every pivot or transition you've gone through—they've all prepared you for this moment.

Will anyone want to buy my program?

If you're able to step back from your fear or apprehension and trust that you have enough expertise to create a program, you may be wondering whether anyone will buy from you.

They will—if you've chosen to provide the solution to a problem your ideal clients are actively looking for. That's the key to choosing a hot topic for your online program.

Your people are out there right now, waiting to hear your message. You need to get crystal clear on who your ideal clients are and what they are willing to invest in, so you can tailor your marketing to them.

When your message resonates with them, they'll buy from *you* because they want the transformation that you, and only you, can provide.

But what about all the competition?

You might be thinking: "There are tons of online programs out there. Hasn't it all been done?"

First of all, if you have competition, it's a really good sign! It means that there is an established demand, and your people are already investing money in solutions similar to yours.

And, here is something important to keep in mind:

The most unique thing about your program is *you*. When you dial in on what makes you or your approach unique, and market your unique message to your audience, the competition will fade away. There is enough space for everyone, and your people will seek your message and decide to work with you because you're *you*.

Will it work for me?

In this book, you'll read stories about how creating online programs changed the businesses and the lives of 20 entrepreneurs.

All of these brilliant business owners overcame their own challenges and struggles to create programs that have empowered them to get clear on their message, reach more people, impact more lives, and enjoy greater freedom.

These entrepreneurs come from a variety of industries and backgrounds, so I hope that in reading their stories, you'll see that harnessing the power of online programs is possible for you, no matter where you are on your entrepreneurial journey.

In addition to information, I hope that in the pages of this book, you'll find a lot of inspiration, too.

How do I actually go about creating my first online program?

Without further ado, here is my six-step process for creating your first online program:

Step 1. Make a decision to create a program.

I mentioned earlier that an online program offers many benefits, not only for you as an entrepreneur, but also for the people you serve and for your family. It empowers you to leverage your time. You invest time and effort up front in creating the program, and then it can reach and transform the lives of many, many people for years to come.

Once you've made the decision to create a program—the foundational piece of your leveraged and scalable business—nothing can stop you. But you have to make the decision. Not next month, not next year, but *right now*!

Once you make that decision, all you have to do next is take action. Follow the steps I outline below to decide on your topic, create your program, market it, sell it, and use it as a launching pad for your high-end offers.

Step 2. Uncover your hot topic.

This might seem a little daunting, right? "Hot topic" sounds so ... exciting! How can you be sure the idea you choose for your program is the right one and something your ideal clients will want to buy?

Here, I'm going to share a powerful exercise for uncovering a topic that brings together your unique life experiences and expertise to guide others in creating transformational results.

One piece of advice before we dig in: don't put everything you know into one single program. Not only is it overwhelming to try to include everything (to the point that you may freeze up because you simply can't figure out how to fit all of it into one offer), but also, it's important to have more information to share if and when you decide to create other programs or trainings.

Earlier in this chapter, I explained why I believe you're already an expert, with enough knowledge to impact the lives of others. Every single experience you've had has led you to this point.

Every success, every failure, every victory, and every trauma has taught you important lessons about moving forward, pivoting, starting over, or expanding on a win.

You've traveled a unique road that no other human being has experienced.

You are the only one in the world with your unique combination of skills, talents, knowledge, and expertise.

There are people all over the globe who need exactly what you know and experienced. They need information only you can provide, explained in a way only you can.

But which information should you share? And in what way?

Exercise: Identify Your Hot Topic

As promised, here's an exercise that will help you identify your hot topic:

Grab a pen and paper and begin writing down your answers to the following questions. Consider this a brainstorming session; don't leave anything out (and be sure to actually take the time to write out these answers—the act of writing helps solidify information and ideas in your mind and gives you a visual you can use to see patterns related to your idea).

First, Let's Identify Your Unique Expertise:

1. Write down all areas in which you have years of experience, personally and professionally.

2. Write down any special training or education you've received.

3. In which areas do you consider yourself more knowledgeable than an average person?

4. List your past jobs, positions, careers, and business experiences.

5. What are you really good at?

6. Are there certain topics about which you can talk for hours?

7. What are your unique talents, gifts, and skills?

8. How do you help people in your day-to-day life?

9. What facts make you, your life, your background, your journey, and your experience unique?

10. And finally, in which areas do you consider yourself an expert?

Second, Let's Narrow Your Topic:

1. What comes easily to you?

2. What if you were given 15 minutes to prepare, and then asked to speak onstage to give advice related to your business? What would you speak about?

3. Can you identify and list some basic steps you take all of your clients through?

4. Write down tasks you complete every day to grow your business, improve yourself, upgrade your relationships, boost your health, or uplevel other parts of your life.

5. Is there a life-changing breakthrough process you took yourself or someone else through that made a huge difference in his or her life/relationships/health/business?

6. Write down five different ideas for topics you could write about or speak on without doing any research.

7. What is one thing you do in life or business that people always ask you about? (For example, "How do you always look so relaxed?" or "How do you manage to get so many leads from networking?")

8. If your ideal client invested in an hour of one-on-one time with you, what questions would you want him or her to ask you? What would you want to work on?

9. What is a common thread you see in your answers from the last two steps?

10. Which one solution would you like to focus on with your program? What transformation or result will your program provide? *Remember, it's important not to include everything you know in one program.*

Finally, You'll Need to Test Your Idea:

1. Research whether people are searching for your topic on Google.

2. Are there other programs or products with this focus? (Remember, it's a good sign if there are!)

3. When you talk about your idea to your current or potential clients, what reaction do you get?

4. When you post on social media that you're thinking of creating a program around this topic, what kind of feedback do you get?

5. When you email your list to ask if they have questions on your topic, what do they say?

At this point, if you're getting good feedback and excitement, congratulations! You have uncovered your hot topic.

If not, then go back to the second task (*Narrow Your Topic*) and see if you can tweak the topic, come up with a new idea, or use a different way to describe it.

Step 3. Promote Your Program.

Once you have the idea for the program you want to create and you know the tangible transformation or result your program can provide, it's time to start spreading the word about it—yes, *before* you create the actual program.

I know. It might seem scary. And maybe even a bit backwards.

But, trust me …

I can't tell you how many times I've seen people come up with an idea for their program and then put a ton of time, energy, and money into creating it, only to *never* sell a single copy.

Let it sink in for a moment. Imagine spending thousands of dollars, and years of your life, to create a program, only to never sell a single copy, no matter how hard you tried, because you created what you *thought* people wanted, not what people actually were buying.

Here's the thing: selling your program before you create it ensures you don't waste time or money creating something no one wants. It ensures there is demand for your solution before you put any effort into making it into reality.

And the best way to ensure you are creating a program that practically sells itself is to sell it *before* you create it.

Which means, you need to start telling people about your program … right away.

When you first start these conversations, you'll find that some people say it's a great idea, while others won't seem interested at all.

At this stage, all feedback is good feedback.

If your ideal clients don't seem interested, ask yourself:

- Am I using their language (the way *my ideal clients* would describe the solution they are looking for in their own words)?

- Am I promising the results that they want and are willing to invest in?

- Am I talking about benefits (how people's lives will transform) or the features (the deliverables like lessons and worksheets)? (Hint: You want to focus on the former.)

If you're not getting the response you hoped for, try fine-tuning the language you use to describe your program, review the way you describe the results it can provide, or even go back to the drawing board of Step 2 and try a different topic.

If, however, your ideal clients perk up and lean in as soon as they hear about your program, then you can move on to Step 4.

Step 4. Sell Your Program as a Pilot.

Once you get the lean-in, *that's* when you sell your program. That's the best time to enroll people.

You don't even need to have all the details at this point … seriously!

I've had a number of clients who've filled their programs before they even named them or put together a single piece of content.

All you need to have in place is the promise of your program (to let your people know what they can expect as a result), the price, and the start date of the program. That's it, really.

When you get the lean-in, it's time to immediately "close the deal." The only opinion that matters when it comes to your program is the opinion of the people who vote with their credit cards.

When someone says, "That sounds very interesting. Let me know when you're doing it," you don't want to respond by saying, "Sure, I'll let you know in a few months." Your response should be, "We are actually starting in two weeks, and you can sign up right now. I take credit cards."

And when that first person pays for your brand-new, not-yet-created program, it creates a "point of no return." Now you *have* to create your program because you have a paying customer and you just got an "advance" (you are getting paid to create your program). No more procrastination or putting it off until next month or next year.

Speaking of paying for your program, my recommendation is to run your new program as a "pilot" at a much smaller introductory rate than you intend to sell your program in the future. This will give you confidence to sell it even though it hasn't been created yet, keep you from getting stressed in case something goes wrong, *and* provide an irresistible one-time offer to your ideal clients.

In my formula, the goal of the pilot program is not to make money; it's to create the content of your program (proof of concept), to guide your participants through transformation, to get their feedback, and to collect success stories and testimonials—because that's what will help you sell your program for years to come.

Step 5. Create Your Program.

Now that people have bought your program, it's time to create it and run it live.

The live element is crucial. I highly recommend creating your program as you go, module by module, while getting feedback from your pilot participants every step of the way. Their feedback will help you fine-tune and adjust your program to make sure it can deliver on its promise.

Once the program is over, you'll know you've created and packaged a step-by-step process that actually helped real people achieve real results.

Step 6. Leverage and Monetize.

This is where things get fun!

Once your pilot is complete and your online program is created and tested with real people, it can easily become the foundation for building a six-figure business and beyond.

You can sell your program from stage, offer it from online webinars, or make it a bonus for your high-end offers.

Your online program can become the foundation for all of your other offers, from one-on-one to group coaching, to VIP days, to masterminds, to events, workshops, and retreats, to done-for-you services.

And that's where you'll start seeing rewards and revenue.

The bottom line:

Your online program has the potential to be at the center of a thriving business, rich with offerings that will change peoples' lives *and* give you the freedom for which you work so hard!

And that's just *one* program.

What if you created two? Three? A dozen?

The sky is the limit!

So even if don't yet have all of the steps, I'm here to tell you: **you are ready to create this reality for yourself.**

You are ready to create you first successful online program.

You *can* do it.

You have what it takes—the experience, the expertise, and the passion for sharing your message.

My clients and I are living proof that moving past fears and reservations and taking action to move toward the entrepreneurial freedom you dream of *is* possible—and rewarding.

It's my sincerest hope that you're starting to see how your program can form the foundation for that six-figure business and beyond … and that you feel empowered and equipped to begin creating it.

On the following pages, you'll read stories from people just like you who share their personal journeys, successes and failures, and lessons learned from creating online programs. You'll hear from a self-proclaimed "misfit," a lawyer-turned-physic-energy-healer, and a heroin addict who became the heroine of her success, to name a few.

Each of them is sharing a special gift with you, too.

Speaking of gifts, get mine …

9 Questions to Ask Yourself to further narrow down your idea for your first program here:

TeachYourExpertiseBook.com/gifts

Chapter 2
The Beauty of Being a 'Misfit'
by Ann Hession

I'm that misfit—a sales expert AND healer!

There have been times in my life when I've felt like a real misfit.

You see, I have what most people see as a pretty strange combination of skills and passions.

I'm a healer. For over 30 years, I have studied alternative and transformational healing work, and I've worked in various related fields for most of my life: massage therapist, life coach, director of a large wellness center, and most recently, energy healer. I love operating in the healing space!

But I also have a passion for entrepreneurship and business—for sales, in particular. I know, right?! A healer who loves sales? That's just weird! Most healers and coaches would rather crawl into a hole than have a sales conversation. But I *do* love sales, the way that *I* do sales. In fact, I've sold millions of dollars' worth of wonderful, heart-based products and services (my own and others') over just the past few years alone.

With my love for healing work and my ability to sell, I built quite a successful six-figure energy healing practice. I was busy doing remote (as opposed to in-person) energy healing sessions, but I was also limited.

I could only do so many one-on-one healing sessions per week. And because my ability to expand my business and income was directly tied to how much time I could put in, there was a cap on my earning potential. The only way I could see to expand was to hire other practitioners to work for me. I wasn't worried about having enough clients at all, but the idea of having to manage a group practice was very unappealing!

That's when I was introduced to the idea of online programs—a whole different way to leverage what I did and the number of people I could help that I'd never even considered.

With a group program, I could teach, coach, and do group energy healing rather than be limited to one-on-one sessions. And, I could do it all online!

It was such a revelation! I jumped right in.

First, I took a good look at my then-current client base. My best healing clients, the ones who love everything I do and refer everyone they know to me, were holistic, naturally minded moms. And one of the biggest things I know many moms struggle with is high stress and anxiety. So, I created a six-week online program called **Calm Mom**, in which I shared my most effective techniques for powerfully shifting stress and anxiety and facilitated weekly group energy healing.

Boom! In just over a month from when I first had the idea to create a program, my pilot was running with 10 moms enrolled!

I loved leading that program, and it was so gratifying and fulfilling to see the amazing results the moms experienced.

So, I marketed the program again, this time at full price instead of "pilot program" pricing.

And it didn't go the way I thought it would. Despite putting a LOT of effort into marketing, finding affiliate partners to help promote it, and creating a wonderful free lead-in to the program, I only had four women sign up.

They too experienced wonderful results, and they loved the program.

I really had to stop and look at what I had created. I enjoyed delivering the program—it was a joy! But was it worth all that time, effort, and expense in marketing it, with so little monetary return?

I was facing the dilemma every business owner deals with at some point (and sometimes, at many points)—to keep going, keep building momentum, keep working at it until I got there, *or to change direction.*

I re-evaluated the entire program: what I loved about it, what it did for participants, what I wanted them to get out of it, and how much I loved helping moms. I thought about how frustrating it was for me that so many moms I talked with about the program loved the idea of it—they were drowning in stress and anxiety and really wanted to do it—but they didn't sign up for it.

39

And I thought of how often, even with the one-on-one healing work I did, the moms would have me work on their kids, their husband, their mom … instead of themselves.

I came to realize that I was fighting a tough battle trying to get moms, who are so committed to taking care of others, to take care of themselves.

I resisted that hard truth for a long time, because I so wanted to make helping and supporting moms the focus of my work. But I had to accept that my target market really struggled to feel okay about investing in themselves and their own well-being.

And it was ironic—the very reason the moms truly needed what I was doing was the exact thing that kept them from doing it!

Just because I wanted to change that for them didn't mean I could— at least not directly.

There's a concept in marketing called "dating" your target market: you pick who you think are your best ideal clients, and go for it full out, like you are seriously dating. And it's exclusive! You don't date (market to) anyone else. You commit fully, with the idea that this might be the one! You "date" that chosen target market, exclusively, for at least six to nine months.

After that period of exclusive dating, if it's not really working, you consider "breaking up" and choosing a new target market, taking into account everything you learned, what you liked about working with the first group, what they loved about you, what they did and didn't seem to value about what you offer, and how much you enjoyed, or didn't enjoy, working with them. You take all that you've learned, wish them well, and move on. Perhaps you move on to a totally different type of client, or maybe it's just a slight course correction … but in every case, it's about following your gut and finding the people you love to work with most.

Reflecting, I still loved the idea of working with moms. I'm a mom myself, and I so loved being able to earn money to support my family by working at home doing something I was passionate about. And that's when it really hit me—I'm not "only" a mom; I'm a mompreneur!

And I'm a *successful* mompreneur.

I've created a six-figure business income for myself, working from home, while raising my kids, and I LOVE that!

All of the sudden, I realized that the part of myself that I was most passionate about, at this time in my life, was that entrepreneurial part of me. Sure, I wanted to help moms, but *moms who are out to create their own businesses*. I love to be able to help them, and other heart-centered entrepreneurs, succeed doing what they love.

 The two sides of me, the healer and the sales lover—came together in a whole new way as everything became clear.

My ideal client is the heart-centered business owner, including (and especially) moms. I get her pain and her commitment. I know how hard it is to try to raise your family and grow your business without losing your mind.

And I love helping people create something they can be proud of *for themselves* in addition to everything they do for their families. I want them to have the flexibility to make family and business work.

I love my ideal client! And I know that, for most of them, the single biggest thing that's holding them back from succeeding in their business is the other thing I love—sales. I can teach them how to do heart-centered, value-based, authentic sales, so they can grow their amazing businesses as fast as they need without having to feel fake, pushy, or salesy, which is exactly what's holding them back, every day.

And I can do that *because* I'm that misfit—a sales expert AND healer! I can not only teach heart-centered entrepreneurs the sales techniques they need, but work with them energetically to clear away, for good and all, the limiting beliefs, blocks, and subconscious limitations they've placed on themselves. I can take someone from being so "allergic" to sales that they almost break out in hives before they even pick up the phone to being connected, grounded, confident, and powerfully able to get all the clients or customers he or she needs, while loving it like I do!

I remember feeling like I just might burst with excitement when it all came together.

Just over a month later, I was running my **Soulful Sales Code: 6-Figure Sales Skills for Your Heart-Centered Business** online pilot program, with 23 registrants, AND ... I had charged three times as much as I had before for the Calm Mom pilot program!

Within the first couple of weeks, participants were having breakthroughs they had no idea were coming, AND they were making sales!

Here are some snippets from the many comments I received from them:

"The very first energy clearing we did in the program made all the difference for me. Although it was done in a group, everything Ann cleared felt like it was just for me. Her intuition was amazing! It cleared up this huge black cloud I didn't even know I was in. That one clearing alone was worth the price of the whole program."

"Before I did the Soulful Sales Code program with Ann, I had no idea how to do sales. I was starting from ground zero. Helping people get over the mindset blocks was huge ... Ann's heart-centered approach steeped in a really deep understanding of sales was such a cohesive and natural way to learn sales."

"Now, I can be present with people and identify where they were in their process. I can really listen, and I know what to ask and what they needed to hear in order to say 'yes.'"

"Sales was so uncomfortable and kind of unfathomable to me. I didn't even know how to start creating rapport with people. Now I can see sales is just a skill, but it's not a skill that's icky, the way it seemed before. It's really just learning how to have a conversation! I can be excited and proud to offer my service, not feel ashamed or uncomfortable to make an offer."

"What I loved about the Soulful Sales Code program was the two-part approach. We did the energetic clearing to clear out inner blocks with the whole group in the live classes, and we had the training videos that helped me understand how sales works and how people make decisions – it was the combination that really made the difference."

"I loved the approach of this program that focused on the inner game as well as sales skills. I've had a lot of sales training before, but the way Ann teaches was really different, relaxed, not like a formula but fluid, and that helped me see sales in a different light, especially how we worked with intention. That was one of my biggest lightbulbs, and I've already seen results from it in easier, more effective sales. In fact, I've closed more sales on the first try than I did before the program. My closing ratio was at 42% previous, and it's 76% during/after the program!"

I believe, based on all my years of experience, that the single most important skill you need to grow your business and make money is sales. When you are conflicted and fearful and hung up about the process of making that sale (and most people are), it's so hard to succeed, no matter how wonderful your product or service is.

Unless you are going to hire a salesperson, which hardly anyone does when starting a small business, *you need to become skilled at making one-on-one sales yourself.*

I also understand that heart-centered solopreneurs and mompreneurs like the ones I love to work with are so averse to sales that it's *painful* for them. They feel so awkward and weird and yucky and pushy. And when you're selling your own services, it's *so* personal!

I get it, and I want you to know that it does NOT have to be that way, even if it seems impossible to you that you could ever enjoy—and be effective at—selling.

If there's one thing I want you to get about sales, it's this: you've been "sold a bill of goods" about sales, and what sales is, and it's NOT TRUE.

Often times, we think that, in order to sell, we have to become someone we're not. Even worse, someone we don't want to be!

Is that how it feels to you?

Here's the thing:

That is the exact opposite of the truth.

What if you could just be you, and make sales, *being you*?

If you like the sound of that, you're going to love this:

Not only is it possible to make sales, LOTS of sales, just being yourself, but it's exactly the most important element *in* sales!

That's right. One of the core principles of success in sales, and of the Soulful Sales Code (and the thing that has helped me personally sell millions of dollars of products and services), is this:

The most powerful and effective thing you can ever do is just be yourself, right here and right now.

So take a deep breath, let go of anything in your head telling you to be someone else, and repeat the following out loud:

"To successfully sell what I do or offer and grow my business as big as I want it, I never have to be anyone other than my own most authentic, aligned, true self—not for one single second. And, to sell effectively, I need sales skills. I can learn the skills of sales, just like I've learned other skills, and use them effectively while being 100% myself, to build a business I love."

To put it another way, *you* are not the problem!

You are perfect.

You just need the skills, so you can use them to build what you want.

Speaking of building what you want …

You're reading this right now because you want to (or are at least thinking about) creating an online program. Right?

Because I have experienced for myself what a powerful process that is, as well as how it can open doors you maybe never would have otherwise even approached, I'd like to leave you with the two most important takeaways I had from that journey:

1. Spend time figuring out your unique offering. Your own brand of weird and wonderful, the unique combination of experiences, passions, interests, and more that make you *you* is the key! For years, I didn't see how my love of sales could align with my love for healing in any way other than to help me get clients. That was great, but there was still a disconnect. Once they came together, though, and I saw how I could use energy healing and sales expertise together to truly transform other peoples' lives, the magic happened, and it's the most fun I have ever had professionally (and that is saying a lot, since I've made a career out of doing things I love!).

2. Give your target market a fair chance. Once you've chosen it, really take it on. Be exclusive with them, and give them everything you have, but then after you've done that thoroughly, be willing to step back and re-evaluate as needed. Note what you learn. Do they really want the things you most want to give? Do you love working with them? Are they willing to invest in what you have to offer? If not, it may be time to move on, but don't regret the dating experience. It will provide you with so much to take to your next one, and honestly, you may have to date a few before you find "the one." All of your dating experiences will prepare you to be ready for the right one once you find it!

And you do need to find "the one," because he/she is waiting for you!

I believe, if you first get really clear on your target market and unique offering, you'll be well on your way to figuring out how to create a program that will help you reach more people and build your business.

* * *

Ann Hession is the creator of the Soulful Sales Code, a program for heart-centered, value-based solopreneurs, mompreneurs, coaches, and healers. Ann has a highly unusual combination of skills—as an intuitive coach and energy healer with over 30 years' experience in transformational healing and a sales expert who's sold millions of dollars of products and services, she's uniquely qualified to help heart-based entrepreneurs transform their relationship to sales, so they can confidently and easily grow their business without ever feeling fake, pushy, or salesy. When's she not helping heart-centered entrepreneurs transform their inner game and discover how "selling" can feel as aligned and powerful as their healing and

coaching work, she's most often found reveling in her flower garden in the summer, reading a good mystery in the hot tub in the winter, or traveling somewhere beautiful to continue her personal and professional growth, because learning and experiencing something new every day keeps your mind and heart young, vibrant, and alive to possibility! That's something she learned from her mom and is grateful for every day. You can learn more about her here: soulpreneursuccesscode.com.

Get Ann's free gift …

Sales Conversation Secrets: 5 Steps to Turn "Tell Me More" into "I'm In!" guide, here:

TeachYourExpertiseBook.com/gifts

Chapter 3
The Hidden Story
by Katja Rusanen

Why?

The question was an open wound that would not stop bleeding.

I was just sixteen, but felt my life had ended in the very same moment my first boyfriend took his.

They said I was a "survivor" of suicide.

I *felt* like a victim of life, left behind to make sense of it all.

Stuck in a new, torturous reality, I desperately wanted to turn back time. With a heart shattered into thousands of pieces, it was so hard for me to accept his choice. I felt responsible, and was full of self-blame.

I should have been there to save him, but I wasn't.

The guilt made me feel like I was constantly being judged by the people around me, too. And in fact, I was. Some of them *did* blame me.

He was gone, and the future had lost its meaning. It felt too painful to even breathe.

My own suicidal thoughts became increasingly louder. They became so intense, that one morning, I walked to a river and stepped out into its cold embrace.

Right then, a glimpse of light entered my dark mind. An image came to me—my older brother who had drowned in that very river two years and one day before I was born. I thought about my parents, and I just could not bear the thought of them losing another child.

I felt love in my broken heart, and it was that love that pulled me back toward life.

My search for meaning began the moment I turned away from the river, seeking a reason to live.

I already knew having a purpose in life helps to keep us going, and it was clear to me that there was a reason things happened the way they did in my life. I just didn't know what that reason was.

I asked myself what my purpose could be. At first, nothing came to me. Everything looked grey and pointless.

Yet I made a decision to move on. I did not want to talk about what had happened any longer. I simply put a smile on my face, and people left me alone, thinking I was okay. Little did they know that the painful memories and guilt did not go away.

After many years, I was eventually ready to start working through the trauma, and later still, to let myself heal.

Then, one day, something I had never even imagined possible happened:

I had finally picked up my thousands of pieces, and I was able to breathe with ease.

The shift occurred when I truly integrated the awareness that *life didn't happen to me; it happened for me.*

For many years, my thoughts created a prison cell that kept me stuck in the past. I had carefully hidden this part of my story away, and because of that, I carried the weight of that deep, dark secret inside me.

Every time it resurfaced in my mind, I would push it away. Still, I sensed that one day, my story would emerge.

Twenty-two years after the traumatic event that changed my life, I completed a fictional young-adult trilogy that is loosely based on my own story. Through the healing power of writing and authentic self-expression, I recaptured the lost pieces of my soul.

And once I shared my story, I felt free!

I gained an understanding of my life from my soul's perspective. Instead of only seeing the emotional pain, I was able to see how the experience had accelerated my spiritual growth and taught me compassion and love. And although I didn't realize it at the time, I see now how sharing my story helped others to share theirs.

That sharing of a story is so important—each of us has a powerful journey, and when shared, it can become an important tool for growth, learning, and upliftment.

This realization became my calling.

You see, in life, we all go through adversities. It's easy to view the darkest moments as a curse that ruins everything. It's a bit more challenging to view them as seeds of spiritual growth.

The truth is, we can choose to see ourselves as a victim of life or the hero of our story. When we choose the latter, we discover the positive lesson we have learned through the experience, and gratitude fills our hearts.

In telling my story, I learned that in sharing your unique, meaningful story and the lessons you learned, *you are serving others*.

From fireside folktales to Super Soul Sunday with Oprah, stories have been used throughout humanity to share what we learn with others. It's easy to remember a good story.

Narrative is of course part of our everyday life, but creating and telling a compelling story that truly connects, transforms, and inspires people to take action can be challenging, and requires specific skills. Craft, structure, and vulnerability are required. So is the willingness to share from your heart and to embrace the power of emotion.

Emotion often plays a critical role in decision making and purchasing behaviors. Potential clients need to feel an emotional connection with you, your business, and your products or services. Your story provides that connection, along with a sense of trust.

It explains who you are, building your credibility, and why your audience should care. It makes you stand out.

In other words, it's your unique advantage when marketing your products or services!

The bottom line:

The life experiences you went through to get where you are now have molded you into the person you are today. The very life events that touched you most deeply can also touch someone else's heart. They can provide hope. They can inspire people to take action and cross the bridge toward their own positive transformation. After all, when you hear someone speaking from a stage and moving others with his or her story, you want to work with him or her, right?

I took the leap of faith to follow my calling in 2012, leaving my banking career behind. I was full of excitement and a desire to serve! I had a beautiful vision of how I could ease the suffering in this world by helping people gain freedom from the blocks to their success, so they could achieve their dreams.

As a Spiritual Life Coach, I began guiding others in transforming their wounds into wisdom, sharing their unique stories, and creating the impact they truly desire.

I also expected things to take off within a year. I kept studying free marketing materials and implementing suggested strategies, but I didn't attract any paying clients.

It didn't take long to begin feeling desperate. Too ashamed to admit that I didn't have any clients and needed help, I ended up spending hours and hours in various training programs, still never really getting the results I desired. And, truth be told, I felt jealous reading others' success stories! It seemed so easy for them, and for me, everything was such hard work!

I started to wonder if there was something terribly wrong with me. That insecurity pushed me to keep trying even harder. I bought more training courses. I was attached to my computer almost every waking hour. Still, I kept hitting the same glass ceiling again and again.

My family constantly asked me when I'd start looking for a "real" j-o-b.

I was distraught. I had such a yearning to share my gifts with the world! Surely, returning to 9 to 5 office work would suffocate a part of me!

My negative self-talk was getting stronger and stronger. I kept questioning why I couldn't make my new business work. I felt frustrated by my shyness to promote my services, and I also blamed myself for wasting time in meditation and spiritual studies instead of pushing even harder. Whatever I did, it was not good enough for my inner critic.

Still, the ongoing urge to make the impact I had envisioned remained and kept me going.

In the midst of all this, I realized I needed to seek answers from spirituality—teachers, books, resources, and Spirit. When I felt ready to give up on life after the devastating loss of a loved one, the spiritual dimension had given me answers. Why wouldn't it now?

I wanted to know the root cause of my struggles, so I could resolve it. I asked, and as the saying goes, *"When the student is ready, the teacher appears."*

From there, I had the privilege of working with many wonderful teachers in various programs. I earned two master's degrees in Spiritual Psychology and Spiritual Science in California.

However, things didn't shift until the right business mentor appeared, too.

Overcoming my fear of investing more money into learning, I joined Alina Vincent's "Fast, Easy and Profitable Online Challenges" program, and eventually, her Rising Stars Mastermind.

First and foremost, it made things so much easier than trying to figure everything out on my own.

I followed a step-by-step formula that helped me ground my work and create a clear structure for it.

I remember the pivotal moment when I realized everything I had learned was starting to work! People started signing up for my first online 5-Day Challenge, and my Facebook group, *Lightworkers Who Succeed On Purpose*, began growing faster than ever.

The 5-Day Challenge I created facilitated more active enrollment into my first online program. I was beyond excited when people said "yes" to the pilot. Combining my spiritual awareness with my pragmatic approach, I guided my first program participants toward their goals.

And my next 5-Day Challenges and programs were so much easier to create!

Alina helped me to identify and clarify my expertise, and then structure it in an online format that more people could benefit from. My own experience of the purposeful unfolding of my story naturally led me to explore the same approach with others, which resonated deeply with my first few clients. With Alina's guidance, I developed that approach into my Client Attraction Story System online program—a step-by-step process for choosing and crafting your own transformational story to attract ideal clients and inspire them to want to work with you.

I truly believe that creating an online program has helped me to grow my business. I can reach more people faster. I now also have more clarity and structure for my offers. I can launch products. I have JV partners. I have alumni from my programs and testimonials that speak to my expertise, which gives credibility.

And of course, I LOVE teaching purpose-driven entrepreneurs how to start sharing their story more effectively by breaking free from their fear of speaking up and overcoming their success blocks. This is a vital step toward achieving the impact and income they truly desire and succeeding *on purpose*!

To illustrate the point, I'd like to share with you what one of my program participants wrote about how I connected with and helped her:

"Before joining the program, I struggled to find the best way to uplevel my marketing and find my ideal clients. Working with Katja, I discovered how my marketing didn't use my powerful stories, and that I needed a clearer structure in order to attract future clients. After working with her, we established my unique story that attracts and connects with my ideal clients, as well as concrete steps on how to use it in my marketing.

Thank you, Katja, for your enthusiasm and your willingness to guide me with my story structure and being so supportive all the way! I felt really heard and listened to with my current issues and struggles. I now feel inspired and excited to share my client attraction story!"

If you'd like to attract ideal clients through your story, just like my client above was able to do, the starting point is gaining awareness: how do you currently relate to it, and what do you believe about it?

This approach is based on two principles of spiritual psychology that I learned at the University of Santa Monica and consider key:

First, *"How you relate to the issue is the issue, and how you relate to yourself while you are going through the issue is the issue."*

And second, *"What you believe determines your experience."*

When sharing our personal stories, especially the vulnerable moments, it is normal to experience doubt, hesitation, and even fear of what might happen should we reveal our struggles. Our inner dialogue might be full of judgement. *"I should have known better, done more, be more."* We procrastinate, hide away, or completely avoid sharing the key stories that attract clients.

That's natural.

To help you overcome that resistance, I'd love to walk you through an exercise I use to help my clients gain greater awareness of—and share—their stories.

I recommend you write your responses in your journal.

Step 1: Tune in. Become more aware of your thoughts and feelings about sharing your story. If you knew you were about to share your story, including its highs and lows, victories and failures, to an audience right now, what would your reaction be? What thoughts emerge in your mind? What emotional or physical reactions surface?

Step 2: Go back in time, and recall the struggles that you have overcome. Think about yourself at the lowest moment in your journey. What were your beliefs about yourself and your situation back then? How did you feel? What did you think? Notice if you have any resistance to sharing this, and be gentle with yourself.

Step 3: Explore the reasons for sharing your story. Become aware of whether your thoughts and feelings change, if you knew sharing your story could help others who might be going through something similar. In what ways would it help people?

Step 4: Bring your attention to the most powerful reason that has emerged for you in the previous step of exploration. This is often called your "Big Why." Imagine an opportunity to share your story and help others on their path. How does it make you feel?

Step 5: Notice any emotional and physical reactions that arise. Are there any blocks and resistances? What support could be useful to you in overcoming them to share your story, if you feel called to? What might your next step be?

Take a couple of deep breaths as you close your journal. Notice if anything has shifted. Acknowledge yourself for your willingness to do this work!

You may have noticed that exploring the reasons for sharing your story helps you overcome the obstacles you encounter when it comes to sharing it.

Remember, *your story matters*. It can create a meaningful and positive impact in the world through its resonance. There are people who want and need to hear it! They want to learn from your experience and insights.

The beauty of sharing your story is that new levels of freedom and authenticity gradually unfold. On the one hand, it is a personal healing journey. On the other, it is an effective way to attract your ideal clients and connect with them on a deep emotional level.

Once you know how to share your story in a structured and strategic way, you will be able to do so with clarity, confidence, and ease.

And, if you're thinking about starting an online program to grow your business, in addition to using your story to connect, this is my best piece of advice:

Allow yourself to get support from someone who has mastered the art and science of program creation. It saves you so much time! You don't need to go through the many stages of trial and error by trying to figure out all the critical components by yourself.

Instead, you can follow a proven formula that brings clarity and helps you to create programs that give results!

* * *

Katja Rusanen is a #1 best-selling author, spiritual mentor, success coach, and creator of the Client Attraction Story System, a step-by-step program for purpose-driven entrepreneurs to craft stories that sell. After working as a supervisor in one of the world's leading business banks, she obtained two master's degrees in Spiritual Psychology and Spiritual Science. She has now dedicated her life to helping clients discover the power of personal stories and create a business they love. Katja lives in gorgeous Marbella, Spain, and loves horseback riding, long walks on the beach, and watching the sunset. You can learn more about her here: www.katjarusanen.com.

Get Katja's free gift …

3 Keys to Telling Personal Stories That Attract Clients and discover the three essential elements to include in your personal stories that will attract your ideal clients, create an emotional connection, and inspire them to work with you here:

TeachYourExpertiseBook.com/gifts

Chapter 4
Stay True to Yourself, No Matter What
by Wendy Petties

For as long as I can remember, I've focused on making myself happy. If there was something I wanted, I would figure out a way to get it. I had big dreams and wanted them to come true no matter what.

I instinctively knew that any obstacle in the way of achieving them could be seen either as a problem or an opportunity. If I could not take control of a situation, then it was not my problem. If I could take control, then I could do something about it.

In other words, I've never believed in just letting things happen by rolling the dice. My happiness is way too important.

I come from an entrepreneurial family, and I am a planner—so, on September 7, 2005, I completed the paperwork to start my company, Simmer, LLC. I chose the name carefully; "simmer" refers to a state or temperature just below boiling point. The boiling point of a liquid varies depending upon the surrounding environmental pressure. I knew even then that someday, I would use my company to create whatever I desired in my life despite any pressures I had to manage, and someday, it would be my mission to help other women do the same.

Now, I always had a side hustle. I have been selling things and information for as long as I can remember. I started facilitating workshops for women, sharing the life lessons and skills I had picked up while earning my MBA and Psychology degree. They wanted to learn everything from how to save money, how to start their own businesses, and how to navigate the often-tricky world of personal relationships. I kept at it evenings and weekends even while working my dream jobs over the years:

- With United Way of New York City, I ran a program that helped nonprofits secure much-needed business support they could not otherwise afford.

- I managed millions of dollars on Wall Street at AIG.

- I helped build leaders as an in-house Executive Coach for JetBlue Airways when it was just a startup.

I enjoyed my jobs and excelled at them (both financially and in my accomplishments), but it was a real struggle to often be the only person of color (and one of the youngest on staff) all while working over 60 hours a week.

One day, a new boss was hired, and his job description seemed to include harassing me. At least a few times a day, he would scream at me, bully me, and try to make me feel insecure and incompetent. I put up with it for a while, struggled, and then fought back … but it was almost six months before I had enough. I sued the company, won, and almost 10 years after first starting Simmer, LLC, I made my side hustle my full-time hustle.

My new dream? To never work for anyone else again.

The truth is, of all the times in my life that I had to change what wasn't working, find a way to celebrate what was, and most importantly, learn how to tell the difference, this was one of the most important.

It was time to officially start running my own business.

The transition was easy at first, because I had experience working in both personal and professional development and had built up a large following over the years. When I told my network that I was launching out on my own, many people reached out wanting to continue working with me. I had more than enough work to keep busy, which turned out to be a blessing and a curse.

It was a blessing because I loved my work. On the personal development side, I helped my clients lead happier lives. On the professional development side, I helped business owners understand how their bottom line improves when their employees lead happier lives.

It became a curse because the work itself kept coming, faster and faster! Word-of-mouth referrals spread, and I was inundated with work. I was soon putting in way too many hours and quickly burning out. Something had to change. It just wasn't fun anymore.

I began researching ideas and learned that creating an online program was the answer. It was a way to serve many more people, give them value, and free up my time, all while making lots of money.

I eagerly dove right in.

First, I bought several online programs to try out the experience for myself and see what my clients would experience if I chose that path. I had mixed reviews. Some programs promised a lot and gave a little. Others had great information, but when I got stuck, there was little support or guidance. Now, I am no dummy, but I was overwhelmed by being left on my own to figure it all out.

I also purchased online programs to teach me how to create online programs. I found that they all basically said the same thing: find out what you are good at, chunk it into small parts, sell it first, and voila! It felt so generic. I was learning from people who were pretty much all the same.

How could that work for me? Everywhere I turned in the marketplace, the gurus are mostly White, West Coast based, and a bit more "woo-woo" than this straight-talking Black woman from NYC.

At this point, after having spent thousands of dollars over a year's time investing in programs while still putting in the same 10-hour workday I had been before, I had the sense to stop and reassess.

I was so frustrated, and definitely not happy. I worried that I would have to give up and go back to a j-o-b.

Then, I realized something: it was *fear* holding me back. All along, in each program, as my disappointments added up, I feared that I'd be treating my future clients to the same disappointment if I chose to go that route with my business.

How could I run an online group program that would get my clients the results I promised, give them the support they need, and still have it be a unique experience for them?

How could I give my clients what I wanted to give them, instead of what I had received so many times?

Every time I signed up for another program, I was left feeling isolated, alone, and like I had to conform in order to be successful. That isn't me, and I was determined to not put that type of pressure on anyone I worked with.

I wanted my program participants to feel confident in exactly who they are (and want to be).

As it turns out, my worries were unfounded. Ironically, it was while working with a client one on one that I realized the need to practice what I teach my clients:

- Be exactly who you are.

- Use the best parts of yourself.

- Remove obstacles in your way.

Having said those very words a thousand times before, it was in that moment that I *knew* I could create a program that harnesses the power of connection, community, and collaboration.

So, I did. I took the best of what I learned from the experts I'd invested in, and I made it work for me. It wasn't easy, but ultimately, it was the best thing I ever did.

First, I dove into all of the information I had gathered and began to sort through it to decide what would work for me, my business, and my life. I asked myself, *"What is my dream? What does it look like? What does it feel like?"*

I made some progress on my own, but I needed some additional support and structure. Enter Alina Vincent.

I met Alina at one of the rare events held on the East Coast, and we became fast friends. We kept in touch, and she suggested that I enter a contest to pitch on stage in front of 400 people at an event that was modeled after Shark Tank. Guess what? I won one of the coveted spots, and Alina was one of the Sharks! At that time, as a certified Sex Educator, I was selling a program called Sex Goddess Bootcamp, in which I taught women how to use their orgasms to fuel their business success. You should have heard the roar of the crowd when I shared how the quality and frequency of a woman's orgasm can directly impact creativity, productivity, and focus!

I really appreciated the direct and straight-to-the-point feedback Alina provided me onstage and afterward. I purchased her Money

Making Blueprint Program, which showed me more and more ways to utilize the content I already had to make many types of offers. By following the steps in that program, I made $6K on my first group program, and five out of six participants hired me for one-on-one work after the program ended. The second time I ran it, I earned over $11K. Alina then invited me to share my successes with her audience at her next live event.

It was there that I decided to join Alina's Rising Stars Mastermind, which gave me even more clarity and a push to actually pull everything I wanted to do and all that I am—all of my life resources and experiences—together into something I am *really* proud of.

I knew I had to create the program I'd always been looking for but never found—one that taught how to create financial freedom and use it to live your dream life.

I still believe strongly that:

- women can be, do and have anything they set their mind on …

- AND that orgasms are a majorly overlooked resource for self-care and support.

But having the money to support your dreams and desires is key, so I knew my work had to focus on that.

My signature online program and live experience is called **UNSTOPPABLE: Turn Your Dreams Into Wealth**—where your mission, should you choose to accept it, is to finally get out of your own way, start taking action, and create a plan to make the money, so you can have the life of your dreams. (As Windy Chien says in *A Year of Knots*, "...with a plan, nothing is insane.")

And, my participants love it!

Like Beth:

"I met Wendy in a time in my life when I was coasting. I was happy ... enough. I was working ... enough. I was fulfilled ... enough. But I wasn't willing to take big chances. I could feel the need for more always whispering to me. When I met Wendy, that whisper became a joyful shout. Working with Wendy during the last year has made me realize how much more my life can be. I don't want to coast or settle or shrug my shoulders and say, 'good enough.'

I am challenging my beliefs about my career, my romantic life, and my financial health. I continue to work with Wendy because I know there is more to do. More to learn. And more to achieve. No more coasting. Of this, I am so happily sure."

One of the areas Beth and I worked on was how to have the type of intimate, personal relationship that she desired—one full of sex, love, laughter, playfulness, and not necessarily monogamy.

I took her through an exercise called **Your Next Step Check In**. In it, I have my clients answer these four simple questions to assess the full picture when they are at a crossroad and need to make a choice or decision to move forward toward their dream.

I believe there are five areas of focus in life: money, relationships, work, health, and fun—and you can create, design, and plan for a dream situation in any or all of them.

Pick one area to start with, and write down your answers to the following four questions.

Ready?

1. **Needs:** What do you *require* (non-negotiable) in this area of your life to be happy?

2. **Wants:** What would be *nice to have* (bonus) in this area of your life, but would not diminish your happiness if you don't have it?

3. **Dealbreakers:** What things would be *absolutely unacceptable* (intolerable) if they did not exist in this area of your life?

4. **Red Flags:** What *signs or warnings* (danger or problem signals) should you look out for in this area of your life?

Take some time to reflect on what you have discovered. Once you answer those questions, you will have a much better picture of what you really desire and can make decisions based on what you now know. Until you can identify the things that will lead you to your dream, there is no way you can plan a way to get there.

Next, you *make a plan*—one that is simple, reasonable, and your very own. It is tailored to you, your experiences thus far, and what you want.

Finally, decide to take the steps you've laid out, knowing that in order to have what you want, you need to do and behave *differently*. (You know what they say about insanity, right? You can't keep doing the same things over and over and expect different results.)

Throughout my life, I have been through chronic pain, multiple surgeries, bankruptcy, infertility, death of loved ones, and depression.

Despite it all, I can honestly say I am living my dream life!

I learned to differentiate between the things I have control over, and those I don't … and I made choices and changes based on both.

Sometimes, the changes I needed to make meant doing more, while other times, it meant doing less. I focused on finding the perfect blend between going for what I wanted and respecting my value system and integrity.

I am, unapologetically, exactly who I am.

And that's how I created a life I really *want* to be living.

You, too, can do the same.

Now, because I know you're interested in creating a program, too, I'd like to offer you some advice based on my own experience:

- ♥ Be yourself.

- ♥ Trust yourself.

- ♥ And decide for yourself what works for you, no matter what others say.

* * *

Wendy Petties, The Happy Life Coach, helps women be financially free, so they can live their dream life. She teaches women how to take control and ownership of their lives by being exactly who they are, using the best parts of themselves, and removing obstacles in the way of their dreams. You can learn more about her here:

www.wendypetties.com.

Get Wendy's free gift …

The Achieve Your Dreams Jumpstart to help you
take the first step toward your dream life here:

TeachYourExpertiseBook.com/gifts

Chapter 5
From Freelance to FREE
by Renae Gregoire

"Hi, Ron. Sorry to have to tell you this, but my child is sick today, so I'll need to stay home."

My stomach was in knots even rehearsing that sentence.

It was 6:30 in the morning, and my son had been up most of the night with fever and, let's just say, "abdominal distress." My husband's schedule was full; I would have to be the one to stay home.

Normally, I wouldn't feel so terrible about having to call in because of something like this, but I worked for a regional accounting firm, and we were in the thick of tax season, which meant 80-hour work weeks (not required, but expected). My then-sick son is also one of three siblings, and his sick sister had kept me home just two weeks before.

Working for an employer, or "the man," even the "regional man," was awful. I hated it. I hated calling in sick for myself or my children. I hated being chained to a desk even when my work was done, and no one had any more to give me. I hated getting the side-eye when I was five minutes late—*as if dead batteries never happened to any of you*, I thought.

This was my life in 2002. I was trapped in a full+-time j-o-b working for the establishment while raising three children under the age of three. It just plain sucked.

One day, while browsing the stacks at a big-name bookstore that has since "given up the ghost," I discovered a book promising to teach me *How to Make $60,000 a Year as a Freelance Writer*. I gobbled it up in just a few hours, my brain whirring and humming all the while. By the time I reached the end, one thought was roaring through my mind: *"I'm a better writer than he is! I can do this!"* (Cocky, I was, back then.)

Per the author's instruction, I invested $20 for a month's membership on Elance (now Upwork). I told myself if I made my $20 back, I'd re-up for another month.

And, well, here I am.

Since that day, I freelanced, feeling so blessed to be able to earn significant money doing something I was naturally good at, *working from home*! Even better than the money, I could finally attend "bring your family" lunch events, show-and-tells, and art walks at my kids' elementary school. I could go on field trips with them and take them to after-school clubs, as well as to sports and music practices. I could pick them up after school, or if dad did so, welcome them home with hugs and kisses at the front door. If I had to quantify, I'd guess that we ate dinner, all five of us as a family, for at least 90 percent of their formative years.

Blessed indeed.

But something inside me shifted as my children turned into young men and women and transitioned to high school. I was weary of writing content for other people. The best way I've found to explain it is to compare myself to a surrogate mother.

An excited, nervous, eager "parent" would hire me, and tell me her story—how she came to her current point in life, what drove her, what she wanted from and hoped for her marketing content—her "child."

She'd hire me, and I'd pour through her existing marketing materials, if any. If she hadn't written content yet, I'd meet with her on a call to draw out all the goodness I needed. I'd research her niche and study her ideal clients. I'd learn her clients' language, so I could "speak" to them naturally, as one would speak to a friend. Then, my client's "baby" taking shape inside me, I'd write. And write. And edit. And write.

And just as a mother's body drains her physical resources to create the miracle inside her, the content being formed within me drained my resources.

Then, finally, my client's "baby," her new marketing content, was born! I'd hand that "child" over to the proud mama, only to begin the entire process again with the next new "mama."

It was exhausting. I was exhausted! This act of birthing, birthing, birthing depleted me.

It was time for something new.

That's when I discovered Amy Porterfield. Wow! Amy, it seemed, had built an empire creating courses and teaching people online. She wasn't birthing other people's children, one child at a time. I wanted to be like Amy!

I bought my very first course back then—Amy's List Builder's Lab—which I think cost me $197. An easy spend, especially when I'd be getting SO MUCH in return! I'd build my list! Then, I'd sell my yet-to-be-created courses—my OWN "babies"—to that list! And, once course sales were rolling in, I'd have the cash I needed to pass on the freelance work, so I could work ON my business! At last!

I'm embarrassed to tell you that today, years later, I still have not completed the List Builder's Lab program. It didn't matter. I was gung-ho; so gung-ho, in fact, that a few months later, I purchased Amy's Courses That Convert program.

Watching the sales webinar for Courses That Convert, I was SO excited. Amy's program would teach me how to create a successful online course! I'd FINALLY be able to stop freelancing! I'd shift into the one-to-many business model that would give me both the money and freedom I craved! OMG, I wanted that program!

But it was expensive— $997! I remember pacing the floor in my bedroom, my husband half-listening, half-reading in bed, waiting for me to finish. As I paced, I spoke aloud, working things out verbally as I tend to do.

"This course is what I've been wanting!" I said, marching one way.

"But it's so expensive." I argued back, marching the other way.

"But I have to do it—how else will I learn to create an online course?" I asked myself.

"Do I have to spend a thousand dollars to figure that out?" came the auto reply.

"But I love Amy's style; she knows what she's doing!" I argued.

"But I'll have to put it on a credit card," I warned.

I stopped pacing.

"Which credit card would I use?" I asked, this time to my husband. I asked him because I didn't yet have a business credit card, and at that point, a thousand bucks was a large, unexpected expense.

"How much is it?" my husband asked.

Oh boy! He's going to say "yes," I thought, answering immediately: "$997."

I waited.

"Put it on our Chase card," he said after a beat, his first of many investments in my dreams.

YIPPEE! I wasted no time. In a matter of minutes, I became the proud owner of Amy's THOUSAND-DOLLAR COURSE—Courses That Convert.

I am course creator! Hear me ROAR!

Maybe I should have mewed instead, because now, several years later, I haven't finished Courses That Convert, either. Even worse, I have repeated that experience with many other courses many times over—and many of those other courses were more expensive than Amy's. Now, in hindsight, it seems that those first two purchases set free my inner piggy bank, making it oh-so-easy for me to purchase more $1,000 … $2,000 … $3,500 courses and programs.

Yet despite all that expense, I still had not created a course. It turned out to be a lot harder than I'd thought. There was all that pre-course research. All that personal development. All that strategizing and planning and preparing—none of which led to an actual course. And to make matters worse, I was still stuck in the surrogate-mommy freelance hell. Now I was now trying to split my time between becoming a course creator AND doing the freelance thing. I was working harder than ever, and earning less than I had in a long, long time.

Then, I met Alina Vincent, and took one of her free, 5-Day Challenges. That Challenge led to me enrolling in her "Fast, Easy and Profitable Online Challenges" program, which led to my purchasing one of her coaching packages, which led to my attending her High Profit Programs event, which in turn led to my joining her Rising Stars Mastermind. This all happened within a few months.

This isn't an ad for Alina. But during her three-day High Profit Programs event, I made more forward motion than I did in all the years that came before, ever since I purchased my first online program from Amy Porterfield. During that event, I funneled my wide swath of unruly ideas into the bones of my first online program. I also met several people who eventually became my first online program buyers. Because of this forward motion—something that felt so good after being stuck for so long—I had no qualms about joining Alina's mastermind, even though it was the most expensive program I'd ever enrolled in.

Has it been worth it? Oh, yeah! Since becoming Alina's student and mentee:

- I created and ran the pilot version of **Blog Your Brilliance**, my five-week online training program. Eleven people joined that pilot, each paying $199.

- I created and twice ran my 5-Day "Express Yourself Marketing Challenge," a fun, lively event that boosted my list.

- The Challenge fed into a webinar through which I enrolled six people in the first run of Blog Your Brilliance, a $997 program.

- I launched and grew my Facebook group—Entrepreneurs on Message—to almost 500 members; it continues to grow.

- My email audience swelled to 1,500 members and continues to grow today.

Those are the stats. They tell one kind of story. The changes within me tell another.

First, in creating Blog Your Brilliance, even though I was scared, even though it was an imperfect pilot on what felt like shaky legs, I finally ACTED. I finally learned the lesson another coach had tried to teach me: that confidence follows action, not the other way around. We often think we need confidence before we'll be ready to act. But, if you think about it, that's backwards. Action comes *before* confidence, not the other way around.

Looking back, I see that the same is true when you're launching an online program. Though the demons of mindset, technology, and money try to get in your way (oh, and they will!), the correct action is not to buy another course; it's to push those demons aside and ACT anyway. The confidence you need will quickly follow, as I discovered when people in my programs began giving me unsolicited feedback like this:

"[Your comments] make me feel confident in my writing, yet also make me look at it with a critical eye ... not just settle for whatever I can bang out. I have always loved the written word, and a goal I set as a child was to become a published author. I am reigniting that flame!"

Wow! Talk about a confidence booster! I never would have received that compliment, nor my client her confidence, had I waited until I had my own "confidence" before stepping forward.

Since then, I've stepped out further and built my email following—action that's resulted in unsolicited email comments like this:

"Hi Renae ... I want to let you know I really admire your courage. I have been following you for a while now, and see how you allow yourself to be vulnerable, which is inspiring. So, thank you :) ... I'm already learning a lot from you and am confident that I will eventually have great success."

I've also stepped out and become more visible—action that's led to invitations like this:

"Hi Renae. I'm assembling a team of experts, and I'd like to speak with you about an opening that you may be a perfect fit for. It's regarding working with TEDx speakers. Might you have availability this week?"

Those testimonials and invitations feel amazing. But the biggest and most profound change that has happened since creating my first online program is that I discovered my WHY.

Before creating Blog Your Brilliance, I had been working for money. Give me money, and I'll write your stuff. Give me money, and I'll have your "baby." I carried on in that way for a good 15 years.

When I finally started moving out of surrogate mode, when I finally began acting and gaining confidence, I began to ask questions. *Why was I doing this work? Why was I writing content for people? Why did I START writing content for people?* It couldn't be all for the money.

It wasn't. I thought back to times when bosses at various establishments asked me to do "writerly things" for them. I edited brochures. Wrote letters. Created and published newsletters. Even while at those accounting jobs, I sent query letters to magazines. I wrote for local chambers of commerce, as well as for local newspapers. Looking back further, I recall my seventh-grade teacher asking me to write a column for the school paper. I remember my English professor begging me to become an English major. Looking back, it was obvious that writing was in my blood.

And then the Internet came. Writing moved online. Anyone could sell writing, no matter their skills. Working as a freelance writer, I read a lot of online content. Too much of it was sloppy and choppy. Little attention was paid to the reader's experience. Does this flow make sense? Who cares?! Publish! Does everything on this site work? Who cares?! Publish! Have 10,246 others said the same exact thing, quoting the same exact people, from the same exact sources? Who cares?! Set that blog post free!

My WHY dawned on me then, and that's when I came alive! That's when I decided enough is enough. I wanted to make the Internet a better place for myself, for readers, for all of us. And I would do so one transformational leader, one web page, one blog post, one email at a time.

Through introspection, which came after I created my online program, after blooms of confidence, I had discovered my why.

Can I say that creating a program has changed my life? A hundredfold, YES.

I stepped up, became visible, and grew my list. I've since followed my passions from content creation, blogging, and editing into new areas such as journaling, creativity, and book coaching.

Today, I look forward to each new day bringing me more joy, insights, clients, and income. And all of it—the passion, drive, and joie de vivre—springs from the shy confidence given to me when I stepped out and created my very first program.

Whether you've already created a program (or three or four), or are thinking about how you can package your expertise and knowledge in a way that allows you to serve many more people while freeing time for your genius work, I'd like to offer you a simple exercise that will help you get clear about your genius work—your passion, your drive, your WHY.

Ideally, I'd like you to answer these questions in one sitting. Then, in another sitting—after your answers have had time to simmer inside you—rewrite your answers in the form of a blog post or an email to your tribe.

Ready?

Part I—The Questions.

1. In terms of work, what do you love doing? What gets you into flow, where all sense of time disappears?

2. Still thinking of work, what do you hate doing? What work makes you procrastinate and easily distractible?

3. Taking a cue from Simon Sinek's book, *Start with Why*, describe:

   a. What you do (your competitors do this, too).

   b How you do it (your process, method, unique value proposition).

   c. Why you do it (your true differentiator, your WHY).

Part II—The Blog Post or Email.

To make use of the work you've just done—and to help you find more of your ideal clients—write your response as an email letter or a blog post, while imaging that you're sitting across the table from someone who greatly respects you. This person has just shared details that ring your "ideal client" button. She's done speaking. She's shared her problems, her passions, and her goals. Now, she's looking to you. She's leaning in, listening. What would you say?

Write *that*.

To make your message as strong and eloquent as can be, read it aloud to yourself. For bonus points, ask a trusted person in your life to read it aloud to you. Before we learned to write, we learned to listen. Your ear is your best editor. Trust it! And then, when your piece is polished, publish it, either to your email list, on your blog, or as a part of your About page. Use it as part of your LinkedIn bio. Publish it on social media. It's your WHY!

If there's one thing I'd love for you to take away from this chapter, it's this:

You don't need confidence to do your work. You only need ACTION.

The confidence will soon follow.

* * *

Content mentor and clarity expert Renae Gregoire is changing the world one outstanding leader at a time. The coaches, consultants, and experts she works with have big visions for transformational change—if only they could create that content! Her work typically involves a blend of strategy and wordsmithing, with a heavy focus on the content experience from the reader's perspective. Renae is also the creator of the Blog Post Inspiration Deck, the Blog Your Brilliance online program, and the Content Coaching Club. She lives in the mountains of North Carolina with her husband and is the proud mom of three grown children. You can learn more about her here: www.ineedcopy.com.

Get Renae's free gift …

The Attract More Clients Ideabook and discover 20 types of marketing content you can use to share your brilliance, grow the "know, like, trust" factor, and warm up a cool audience here:

TeachYourExpertiseBook.com/gifts

Chapter 6
Is Fear Holding YOU Back?
by Larissa Popov

Since I was a child, I knew I was a healer.

The daughter of two schoolteachers, I naturally pursued the rigorous academic path to become a naturopathic doctor. Simultaneously, my spiritual journey brought me into a leadership role in my community—to a path of service.

I truly loved my craft; it was very much aligned with my spiritual values.

Upon entering the entrepreneurial world after eight long years in academia, the naïve idealist in me held fast to the old adage *"If you build it, they will come."* But despite my best intentions, and everything I *had* built, *they* were not coming!

After several uncertain years in business, I continued to carry the burden of massive student loan debt. I lived hand-to-mouth, working part-time jobs to make ends meet. I was also beginning to question whether choosing that particular career and starting my business was a mistake.

I distinctly remember the moment it all came to a head.

I was standing in a coffee shop looking into my wallet when I realized I had six dollars to last me the rest of the week. There I was, a highly educated, highly competent, hard-working healthcare professional who was really good at what she did … yet buying a coffee had become a major financial decision!

I saw others in my field thriving with waiting lists of clients, yet I lived in constant uncertainty—always wondering when my next client would show up, or how I would find him or her.

I just couldn't understand why others were making it, but I wasn't! Was there something wrong with me? Was I destined to fail?

After a lot of honest soul-searching, I realized the truth:

I was afraid.

I was afraid if I shared my life's work that I was so passionate about, no one would want it. I worried that people wouldn't be interested in what I had to say, and even worse, that it would act as proof that I didn't matter. I was not willing to face the rejection. And the fears didn't stop there.

I was afraid to market myself. Afraid that, if I put myself "out there," I would be judged or criticized for being salesy, or for being a fraud. I was even afraid I might get so busy, I wouldn't be able to handle the workload!

I was afraid to let money IN!

After all, I am a healer, not a businesswoman!!

Despite that fact, though, I knew exactly what I needed to do to bring in more business. I just couldn't bring myself to do it, because it felt too scary and out of integrity. I was so concerned about providing a ton of value, I barely thought about receiving compensation for all the value I delivered.

After a lot of self-reflection, I realized that my own beliefs about money and business were stopping me from having what I really wanted.

Eventually, when I got tired of trying (unsuccessfully) to do it on my own, I finally found the courage to enlist the help of a mentor—a business coach who facilitated the inner work necessary to change my relationship with money, marketing, and selling. That helped me focus my actions to ensure that they were authentic and in alignment with my values.

Within a couple of months, I doubled my client numbers, raised my rates, and created my first program!

As time went on, I continued to align my actions more and more with what I really *loved* to do the most, which was to help people get out of their own way so they could realize their potential and be a powerful force for change in the world. I also finally realized that I had the power to make the money I wanted to make … and I had the tools to show others how to do the same.

Over time, my business evolved as I was called to bring together my diagnostic mind and my business experience with insight and intuition to provide a uniquely holistic approach to business!

Now, I've had the great privilege of facilitating transformations for thousands of people. I'm making more money than I ever have in my life, and I'm following my divinely guided path: doing what inspires me—what I'm passionate about—what makes me feel like an angel every single day!

And I am on a mission to simplify the process for heart-centered coaches, healers, and service-based professionals to become strong, confident, forces for good who make money (YAY!) by getting out of their own way and taking focused, aligned, and strategic actions that bring in a consistent flow of clients and income!

I believe when money gets in the hands of good people who follow their unique and divinely guided path, those people will do great things for many more, and leave a lasting legacy on this planet.

To that end, here's how my business evolved into online programs:

After I had been working with one-on-one clients for a while, I realized how much time and energy was required of me. I knew that, in order to reach more people, I needed a way to leverage my time *while* growing my business.

I needed to create an online program. I knew I wanted it to help heart-centered business owners to stop hiding, feel comfortable in their own skin, and show up confidently and authentically in their marketing, so they can showcase themselves as the experts and authorities they are!

Even though I knew it was the next logical step in my business, I was filled with concerns—most of all, how I was going to deliver a powerful transformation that would benefit many people without my direct presence and ability to intuitively hone in on a person's individual needs.

I decided to keep moving forward, despite my fears.

As I worked on the program, I found myself wanting to pack everything I knew into each module, to make sure I was delivering enough value and that participants would achieve the transformation I wanted for them.

I also found that I was resisting the need to just finish and run with it, because I wanted to get it "just right."

Every day, I would get new ideas and insights, and I would continue to revisit, rework, and tweak the content. I had a strong feeling that the program needed to be great (read, perfect), so when I put it out into the world, it would give my clients amazing results and be profitable for my business.

It was a process, to say the least, and I learned a lot!

First, I learned I *can't* replicate the one-on-one coaching experience in an online program, nor was that even the goal.

An online program is a different level of support than one-on-one coaching, and therefore, requires a different approach. The thing is, there are certain universal experiences and steps my ideal clients need to take, and my program is most effective focused on those essential foundations.

Something else I learned (through trial and error!) was how to edit and avoid packing too much into every module. In retrospect, I realize my need to pack in as much awesome content as possible—and all that constant tweaking and changing—was to "prove" the value. When I really got honest with myself about it, it was coming from not feeling "good enough" (as in, I am not good enough).

After running my pilot, participant feedback helped me realize that more information *isn't* better! It actually becomes overwhelming and can make clients feel discouraged or defeated when they can't absorb or take action on all of it. In fact, it's better to focus on a more specific outcome for your program, and provide achievable baby steps in each module, so your participants feel a sense of accomplishment and confidence as a result of completing them.

After my pilot, I ended up removing a huge portion of the program that really didn't belong, which I then used to create a separate online program!

Having created an online program has enhanced my business in many ways. It has allowed me to introduce my work to a new and bigger audience, many of whom have gone on to continue working with me in one-on-one or group coaching programs.

Whether I'm in conversation on social media, in an interview, or even in social situations, being able to refer to my **Own Your Brilliance** online program brings me a feeling of confidence and accomplishment. It's a tangible expression of my authority and expertise!

It has also been so exciting to experience the freedom of passive income—leveraging my time and serving more people in an accessible way that still delivers so much value!

But the most satisfying part by far is watching my clients get results from our work together.

For example, one was a holistic practitioner who had already taken a lot of business/marketing training that hadn't translated into the full practice and financial wealth she was hoping for. She was attracting clients who weren't very committed and didn't appreciate what she had to offer, which was very discouraging. She felt like a valuable resource being underutilized, yet at the same time, she was tired and overworked!

When we started working together, we discovered that she'd been hesitating to raise her rates for a long time. She was giving away a lot of value without being compensated for it, and spending a lot of her time and energy on actions that weren't bringing in the clients and income she really wanted.

We started our work together by uncovering and clearing the limiting beliefs around money, her sense of self-worth, and taking action in her business—all of which were getting in the way of her success. Then, we refined her messaging, so she could communicate her value in a way that would resonate powerfully with her soulmate clients. Finally, we created a clear, focused, and strategic plan that she could take consistent action upon to create a continuous flow of new potential clients.

As a result of our work together, she's raised her rates, expanded her reach, and is getting fully booked more consistently! She feels good about her business, and best of all, she's filling her practice with the kind of clients who appreciate the value she provides, are committed to getting results, and willing to pay her at the rates she charges. All of this allows her to experience the pleasure and rewards of doing the work she's been called to do.

If I can do it, and my clients can do it, so can you!

You too can "Own Your Brilliance," so you can create a profitable and sustainable heart-based business that is an authentic expression of who you really are and in alignment with your values.

To do so, there are five key foundations you must have in place:

Key Foundation #1: You need to feel comfortable being visible.
When you are incredibly comfortable in your own skin, the people who are meant to work with you are effortlessly drawn to you, and you leave a great impression! You need to be seen and heard not only for everything you have to share with the world, but also for your very presence, as that alone can catalyze transformation in others.

Key Foundation #2: You need to know exactly how to talk about your work in a way that speaks to your soulmate clients and gets them curious and interested to know more. Your messaging is so important, because ultimately, it can mean the difference between engaging and enrolling clients and not!

Key Foundation #3: You need to feel comfortable with who you are in your marketing and selling. There needs to be a fine balance between finding your own unique voice that feels natural and loving while being influential, empowering, and intentional! If you ever feel pushy, salesy, or manipulative—if you create that impression unintentionally, or even if you're simply *afraid* of being that way—you'll experience tension in your mind and body, causing you to act in an unnatural way. That tension creates a disconnect between you and your audience, because you've lost touch with your own self and what makes you attractive, inspiring, and compelling!

Key Foundation #4: You need to feel clear and confident in the value you offer your clients, so you can charge your worth, feel good about receiving money, and maybe even raise your rates! I've seen too many heart-based business owners who intellectually know they have lots of value to share, yet act in a way that tells a different story. (For more insight, complete the exercise below).

Key Foundation #5: You need to share more of YOU in a way that showcases your unique brilliance, style, and personality. The reality is that promoting your business is a vulnerable act, especially when you've put your heart and soul into it. The more you can connect and build meaningful relationships in the unique way that only you can, the more you will not only build an audience of potential clients who can't wait to work with you, but also attract the kind of people who love you just the way you are—and isn't that THE BEST?!

I'm here to tell you that, without question, your work IS valuable!

The idea is to know how to communicate in a way that ensures your soulmate clients really "get it," and that inspires them to take the next step with you.

As I mentioned earlier, that *need* to prove our value is one of the most common and pervasive challenges we ALL face.

Here are some really common ways that doubting your value, or the value of your products and services, shows up in your business:

1. Over-giving your time, energy, or service.

2. Undercharging for (or discounting) your products or services.

3. Feeling fear/doubt around raising your rates—questioning whether people will pay your new rates.

4. Perpetually wanting to take more training or uplevel your credentials in order to be seen as a credible authority.

5. Having a tendency to overpromise, embellish, or exaggerate your accomplishments or the results your clients achieve.

6. Diminishing or dismissing the value of your programs, accomplishments, or results you deliver, or feeling uncomfortable talking about them.

7. Overloading your sessions/programs with too much content.

8. Perfectionism: tightly controlling the variables or postponing completion of certain business actions because they're "not ready yet."

9. Procrastination in the form of avoidance, resistance, feeling stuck, confused, overwhelmed, or distracted around making offers, raising your rates, getting in front of a larger audience or "tooting your own horn"—any action that could potentially lead to more clients and income!

10. Rejecting or delaying recognition and appreciation in the form of support, resources, or money from others.

Can you relate to any of these?

When you're working on your online program, it's important to self-reflect on the emotions that are driving you. Acknowledge and love yourself for any feelings of pressure to "get it right" and prove that it's valuable. It shows how sincere and committed you are to helping people, which is so beautiful!

Rest assured that your knowledge and experience IS valuable, and the greatest service you can do for the participants in your program is to help them feel a sense of accomplishment and confidence in completing a series of small steps.

Don't be afraid to start at the beginning and keep things simple, because when we live in the world of our own expertise, we have a tendency to believe that people want more advanced knowledge, when what they really need is to put the foundations in place.

When you're planning your modules, I recommend starting with the end in mind: what is the action you want your participants to take by the end of that module? Design the module to *only* provide the information necessary to accomplish that action step.

When you follow this plan, you'll realize that you actually have a whole lot of value to share, and you might even discover you've got enough material for two to three more programs!

Your online program is an evolving creation. Whatever your program is now, it's going to change as you gain more experience delivering it and getting feedback from your participants, so it's important to release that feeling of pressure or attachment to having it all figured out right off the bat.

As you gain more experience with it, it will only become more aligned with your vision and deliver even better results for your clients, so know that where you are right now is exactly where you need to be, and it will all unfold in divine timing!

* * *

Larissa Popov is a Divine Business Mentor and creator of the Own Your Brilliance program for heart-centered business owners. With a combined 35 years' experience as a graduate school instructor, spiritual teacher, and former naturopathic doctor, Larissa merges a deep inner wisdom and intuition with clarity, logic, and a strategic business mind to take her clients from wondering if they can make it in business to record-breaking revenue! When she's not facilitating inspirational workshops or supporting her clients, you can find her in a contemporary dance class, making music, or concocting a delicious new dish. Learn more about her here: innerfreedomarts.com.

Get Larissa's free gift …

Connection Charisma Quiz to discover your unique client-connection style and receive a personalized report that reveals the special gifts your soulmate clients love about you, the specific challenges you face that can push clients and sales away, *and* a custom toolkit to bring more presence, people, and profit into your business here:

TeachYourExpertiseBook.com/gifts

Chapter 7
From Heroin to Heroine—Finding Your North Star
by Johanna McClain

The practice of yoga has given me strength of character, a deeply personal (and healthy) relationship with myself, and a kinder, more compassionate view of others.

I suppose it's no wonder, then, that it would become my true path.

I entered my first yoga class, an elective, when I was in college in the early 70's following my calling to be a teacher. Things were going great; I was a special education major, and for the first time in my life, I felt a true connection to "self." The combination of these two aspects of my life replaced my need to be perfect—that drive to win and be admired became a distant compulsion.

Then, I met a boy.

I gave myself over to love/lust and marriage. Things could have been okay, except he came home from Vietnam a heroin addict. Not one to be left out, and always one to walk on the wild side, I too became an addict. It wasn't until I was pregnant, knowing I needed to get clean to save my life and the life of my baby, that I decided to leave my husband and move back home to get help. Unfortunately, that was not the end of my addictive behavior. I went on to abuse cocaine, and then, once rid of the cocaine addiction, endured many years of alcohol abuse and cigarette addiction.

God must have decided I had something to offer, because at the age of forty and with the help of an angel, I finally had my fill of substance abuse and began a 12-step program. I got clean and sober by facing up to the fact that the demon looking at me was me.

I came to get to know her—my demon—as a scared and confused creature. I learned how to open my heart to her pain and find a path toward love and forgiveness.

I'm not sure what unknown forces are at play when we lose that sense of "self," as I did, or why we allow the demons of self-doubt and self-destruction to come for extended visits. I suppose there are a number of people and/or circumstances we can blame. But for me, looking back, despite the pain I brought to myself and my family, I know I was meant to take that exact journey.

It was during this time of recovery that I remembered my love of yoga and renewed my practice of it. I was introduced to a gifted yoga teacher who helped me find my connection back to self. That gift became my motivation to pay it forward: if I could help just one person, like my teacher helped me, I would be happy.

So, I began my training as a certified yoga teacher in the early 2000's, while operating my advertising agency that I had opened four years prior.

In 2008, I added coaching to my business, and it was very successful. For the next ten years, I taught yoga as a sideline passion in private spaces and yoga studios. Then, I decided I no longer wanted to be anchored to my weekly commitment, so I took a sabbatical.

After a few months of not teaching, though, I realized how much I missed the personal connection with my students, and watching them find a deeper connection to themselves.

How could I have my cake and eat it, too?

That was the question, and in 2019, divine guidance answered it, clearing the way for Not Your Daughter's Yoga® to emerge. I was shown a virtual yoga studio where women 50+ could come together to practice in the comfort of their homes.

I became very clear on the fact that yoga is my true north, and teaching yoga is my passion and purpose. Once I surrendered to those truths, I set out, at the age of 67, to start a new business.

It has taken quite a few years and different attempts at finding my true path. After years spent attempting to bring my former life as an advertising agency owner and business coach into a completely new virtual yoga business (in other words, attempting to force a linear square peg into a flowing circular hole!), I realized I didn't need to leave *anything* behind.

I needed to create a program that was easily accessible to women my age AND super affordable, so it would be an easy "yes." Since I had been using technology in my businesses for years already, I could see how it could all unfold virtually.

Once again, my biggest challenge was me. I needed to set aside my age and weight insecurities in order to show up and teach! And the only way to do that was to prioritize my "why" over my incredibly critical "ego."

Once I was able to do that, things began falling into place.

I met Alina Vincent in a networking group when she was running a very successful photography business. She did my first professional headshots for my business, and since that first "yes," I have said several more to her over the past few years. I have watched and admired her as she moved into creating the hugely successful business that she now has. Having now known her for years, and having experienced how her guidance and mentorship helped me in my previous business, I knew she was the perfect person to support me in taking the leap I wanted to take with the yoga studio. I trust Alina 100%, having seen her heart and commitment to her clients before, and knowing beyond a doubt that her advice, wisdom, and leadership leads to success. So, it was go time!

Following Alina's guidance to do market research before creating a program, I interviewed 22 women in my target market audience and was able to get clear about what they wanted from a program *and* how it could most benefit them.

Armed with that powerful information, I was able to move forward confidently.

I began offering live online classes via **Not Your Daughter's Yoga®** in June 2019, and am thrilled to have received great feedback from my student practitioners, like the following:

"I love attending Johanna's classes! She quickly assesses individual capabilities and provides tailored suggestions on how to modify a pose to fit those capabilities. Her enthusiasm and engaging style make attending her classes a tremendous pleasure! I really appreciate the flexibility of being able to attend a class "live" or attend anytime that I want through the recorded videos. My meditation practice has greatly improved as a result of the breathing techniques that Johanna has taught us and it's amazing how she is able to provide helpful and sometimes very subtle posture corrections for yoga poses via video!!" - Pam Daniels

"'Stitch your core!' This has become a steady mantra for me as a result of taking Johanna's virtual yoga classes. Johanna said it early on in one of my classes, and I say it to myself all day long now! Johanna is an outstanding yoga instructor, teaching the poses and principles of yoga in a way that my body and mind finally get. And, I love being able to do it in the grace and ease of my own home, in my PJ's if I want, with my kitties nearby. I can tell my posture is improving and the morning aches and pains have diminished. I totally recommend NYDY!!" - Cindy Yantis, Writer

"Johanna is the consummate yoga instructor! She has helped me with some yoga poses that I had difficulty in understanding where, in my body, it was helping and benefiting. As a result of her instruction, I have more flexibility and more range. She is extremely

patient and caring in her yoga classes. I have been doing yoga off and on for close to 15 years, and since going to Johanna, I have benefited tremendously!! Namaste! Thank you, Johanna!" - B.R.

"I really enjoy being a part of the NYDY community and love the convenience and positive impact of the NYDY format and process! Johanna is a truly gifted yoga instructor and is able to expertly guide the class while offering personalized adjustments for all levels of experience and ability. She sets a beautiful tone and intention at the beginning of each class, and gently encourages us to open our heart, get grounded, and challenge our body and soul to fully experience the transformational power of yoga." – Ferrell Marshall

With all of the positive feedback like this, I am encouraged on a daily basis to build on my program, adding virtual retreats, workshops, and so much more. And without the limitations of a physical studio, I am able to reach more women than I ever thought possible from my home studio.

If you're ready (or even if you don't think you're ready) to dive into the program pool, here are a few things to consider:

1. Get clear (*really* clear) on your why. Know what it is that you're up to. Know what difference you will make, and why making it is important to you. This is your North Star.

2. Surround yourself with like-minded entrepreneurs and trailblazers like yourself. So many times, we allow well-meaning friends and family members to darken our sky and dim our North Star. They might mean well, but don't listen to them!

3. Look to experts, like Alina, who have created successful online programs that have changed peoples' lives and businesses already. Since we are usually not our best advisors (I often have to send my mental business partner packing), this is a life- and business-changing decision.

4. Be willing to be vulnerable. This chapter I have written is a great example…this is the first time I have shared my story to anyone outside of my circle of close friends. I'm sharing it now because I hope it will help or inspire you to "take the leap," too.

5. Love yourself that much! It's inside-out work; yoga taught me that. Go deep into that place of truth—your heart—and listen carefully.

All of the contributors in this inspiring book wish you joy, happiness, and huge success! As you pursue your dreams and set out on your own journey, remember to listen to your heart and never lose sight of your North Star.

***

Johanna McClain spent most of her career in advertising and marketing as a successful, trusted advisor, advertising agency owner, and business coach. The breadth of her experience and knowledge, driven by the undercurrent of yoga, brings clarity of purpose, guiding principles, and a solid foundation to Not Your Daughter's Yoga®. You can learn more about her here: www.nydy. life.

Get Johanna's free gift …

one month of FREE virtual yoga classes by going here and using the code RSB30 at checkout:

TeachYourExpertiseBook.com/gifts

Chapter 8
Taking on Your Inner Critic
by Ahulani McAdam

Before I became an energy healer and spiritual mentor, I was a successful environmental and children's rights lawyer in New York City. I had a beautiful loft in Soho, an adorable daughter, and a life that pretty much looked like something out of a magazine.

Then, in my late 30's, that life took a 180° turn; I was diagnosed with what was thought to be ovarian cancer.

Up until that exact moment, I was someone who would have gone straight to the hospital and turned myself over to the doctors. I knew nothing about alternative medicine and thought all religion and notions of God and Spirits superstitious nonsense.

However, this time, for reasons I still cannot fully explain, I did not go to the hospital. Instead, I went on a profound spiritual and healing journey, studying and experiencing many different healing techniques.

I experienced a shamanic initiation and encountered an angelic being, and, nine months later, I was completely healed. Most importantly, the focus of my life had changed completely.

From then on, I only wanted to bring Spirit, healing, and love into people's lives. I gave up my law practice and advocacy work. I devoted myself to doing the deeply personal clearing work I needed to become a pure channel of love, light, healing and truth. I studied with master healers, spiritual teachers, and channels.

And eventually, I began to give spiritual readings, teach classes, and do energy healing myself. I helped my clients connect with their Higher Self, angels, and spirit guides—their own inner guidance. I loved steering them through processes to get their lives into balance, to heal, and to find and follow their dreams!

As with most healers, it didn't matter who came to me or for what reason; everyone who sought me out experienced profound healing. I welcomed anyone who came my way. I began receiving invitations to lead workshops across the country and abroad. My business thrived, and all was quite well.

I didn't anticipate being asked to pivot again.

Then came 9/11. I left New York City and moved to a small town on the Northern California Coast. I had a small practice with a few sporadic clients, relying only on word-of-mouth marketing and an occasional flyer to draw in new clients. I did sessions over the phone with my old clients as well as in person with new ones, but I was frustrated because I was not reaching enough people to support myself financially. Nor was I making the impact I wanted.

Despite hiring business coaches and learning to create and sell comprehensive packages instead of seeing people every now and again, and although I did eventually start making enough money, I felt frustrated and unfulfilled; I still wasn't helping enough people.

I knew the Internet was the way to go to increase my reach, but as is the case in many rural communities, there was no highspeed connection where I was.

Reluctantly, I left my quiet country life and moved to the San Francisco Bay Area where I knew more people would be receptive to my message and there would be plenty of tech support! I also began thinking about ways to *leverage my business* to have a greater impact and create passive income as I lessened my workload.

I thought about the legacy I wanted to leave, too. I realized the biggest impact I could have would be to empower women in leadership roles who shared my vision of a more loving, healthy, and equitable world. Women who were leading the global shift in consciousness—the moving away from old dualistic, paternalistic, and hierarchical paradigms to Oneness and Love.

I decided the best way to reach these beautiful people would be to create and offer online programs that would help them confidently move forward to manifest the enormous changes they wanted for themselves and the world.

While the idea of an online program was compelling in the abstract, when I actually began to create one, I came up against what felt like an insurmountable obstacle: I am an intuitive healer who gets downloads in the moment. In my sessions with people, everything happens spontaneously depending on who is there and what is going on. I tune into and interact with energy. I see colors, Spirits, and Angels. I feel conversations with plants and animals. I grok universal concepts and inter-weavings of history. I funnel all that vast non-verbal numinous awareness into tiny words for humans to easily understand. Little did I know that these great gifts would turn out to be my biggest challenges in creating my first online program!

I struggled to try to make my work look like a regular college course in a PowerPoint presentation. I tried to look corporate. I even picked a red, white, and blue color scheme! My lawyer self suddenly appeared and started fighting with what she called "the woo woo." I was miserable. I could not figure out how to take information that was so alive for me and my clients, that was so individual and personal, and turn it into what I thought had to be a left-brained, done-ahead-of-time, logical outline. I had no idea how to put what I did into slides, much less imagine how those slides could deliver the transformation I was promising my clients … and that they were paying for!

I was extremely frustrated and discouraged. I blamed myself. I wondered what was wrong with me that I couldn't seem to master this apparently simple task. The worse I felt about myself, the harder I tried. Finally, I broke down and confessed to my coach. She said, "You don't need to do a PowerPoint presentation to do an online program! There are many formats to choose from depending on what serves you and your audience best. Why don't you just try recording live group calls on Zoom. There, you can be as spontaneous as you like!"

She also suggested I narrow my focus to help people heal their Inner Critic, specifically. I felt resentful. Didn't she realize that was just a small part of what I was capable of? I helped people awaken to their Divine Nature! I helped them heal cancer instantly! The Inner Critic seemed like such "small potatoes" given all I had to teach and heal. Then, she said something that stopped me in my tracks: "You are always your ideal client, you know." Somewhat akin to, "You teach what you need to learn." This truth hit even closer to home. I had to look closer.

Underneath it all, the thing that had been holding me back at every turn in creating my online program was my own Inner Critic. I had spent so much time and energy engaged with the doubts, fears, and self-criticism that kept coming up that it felt like I was constantly taking a half step forward and three steps backward. I needed to take her advice to heart.

I created an online live call series in a group coaching format, and it was tons of fun, because it was more in line with who I am and the way I like to relate. Most importantly, healing began as soon as people signed up for the course. (There was not one single PowerPoint slide, by the way.) By the third week, the members had experienced transformation beyond my wildest dreams!

I was challenged to go far beyond what I had known before, but I found that all the intuitive "stuff" worked perfectly in the live online format. And there were definite advantages. People were more open and vulnerable sooner than I had ever seen in an in-person workshop. Their heart connection with me and the other attendees was *even stronger and happened almost instantly.* Their intention for the healing of each other was extremely focused and powerful. There was a synchronistic effect that boosted the healing power of each class. We were all surprised and ecstatic!

Although it was a struggle at first to settle on what to do and how to do it, creating my first online program gave me the assurance that I *could* do more. And, once I found a format that worked well for me and my clients, I had the confidence to develop the program further. I also saw how **Healing Your Inner Critic** (my online program) was a lynchpin to helping me create the impact I wanted with the heart-centered entrepreneurs I serve who are changing the world.

Imagine the energy that is freed up when one person breaks free from the mean or discouraging voice in his or her head! The work my clients are doing in the world has become the legacy I wanted to leave behind. My business has become something I am proud of—something I want to nourish and grow. Since I have embraced the amazing benefits of social media, I am reaching far beyond the people who already knew me. I am enjoying learning and using new technologies. I can confidently work with large groups of people, knowing that healing for one benefits *everyone*.

I now know that the reach and impact of the online programs I create are only limited by my own willingness to grow. And for that to happen, I needed a supportive mindset. I needed to transform my own paralyzing Inner Critic into my own custom-made Inner Support Team!

Ultimately, the *most* meaningful part of this journey of transforming my in-person spiritual healing practice into a successful online platform has been my own personal growth. Creating my online program has given me continuous opportunity for the development of my own soul. The exciting truth is that my true motivation turned out to be different than my initial goals. As strange (or "woo-woo") as it might sound my real motivation all along was to *remember my connection to my own Divine Nature and the rightness of its unique expression.*

I also love that my programs contribute to making this world a better place for everyone.

An unexpected delight is that the online aspect puts me in such loving contact with passionate and creative people around the world, who are shining their own light so brightly!

I believe every person who is paralyzed by thoughts about themselves equals one part of creation that is not expressed. Anna, one of the participants in my first program, Healing Your Inner Critic, exemplified this. Because she was so paralyzed by low self-esteem, she never showed anyone her exquisite artwork. She had grown up with a mother who criticized her constantly, from early childhood on, for being "stupid and clumsy"—for not being the pretty and popular daughter she thought she deserved. As you can imagine, Anna was deeply hurt by her mother's judgment. Although she had always been a gifted artist, her lack of confidence in herself kept her playing very small. Outside of the classroom, no one ever saw her work. Although in her sixties, she told us that for her whole life, every time she looked in the mirror, all she saw was an ugly and a hopeless failure.

After the second week of the program, Anna reported that while passing a mirror that morning, she heard a loud voice in her head that said, "You are so beautiful. I love you." She was stunned. We (the community we established in my program) joined her in tears of happiness as she described her transformation.

The following week, she explained that, while writing in her journal, she felt connected to the voice of God's Love inside her.

Finally, a few months after the program ended, she began showing her artwork at a local gallery. She credits this transformation to the healing she experienced in Healing Your Inner Critic.

Because so many of us battle inner critics, I'd like to offer you the following exercise designed to help you begin transforming your inner voice of self-hate into one of self-love. Anna called it "instrumental" in beginning her healing, and my hope is that you too can use it to nurture a better understanding between yourself and your own Inner Critic. Consider it the beginning of your journey toward transforming the negative, scary, paralyzing voices into the support you need to shine your own light as brightly as you can!

The Sacred Dialogue Exercise

Recommended Materials:

- A large newsprint drawing pad 18" x 24" or bigger*

- Fat felt-tip markers (colors are fun) or crayons**

- A pen or pencil.

- A candle (optional)

- A quiet uninterrupted half hour or longer (turn off your phone!)

* In a pinch, any paper at least 8"x11" will do.

** You can use the pen or pencil, but it is much more effective to give the non-dominant hand something easy and child-like to use.

Activity:

- Light your candle.

- Set your intention to make a connection with your Inner Critic.

- Say or write a prayer if you like. What is it you need help with? Be sure to state it.

- With your dominant hand, write:

Dear Inner Critic,

I want to help make our relationship better. I promise you I will try to be open to hearing what you want to say to me, no matter what. I will not make you wrong. I will try not to be defensive.

- Now write: Who are you?

- Pick up the marker or crayon with your non-dominant hand and just let it write its answer. Whatever comes is fine. Don't worry about spelling, etc. Go slow and let the hand write, not your head.

- Let that answer in.

- Now, with your dominant hand, pick up the regular pen or pencil and write, "Why are you so mean to me?"

- Pick up the fat marker with your non-dominant hand and let it answer.

- Continue having a question-answer dialogue in this manner. Suggestions of questions to ask: What do you want? Why are you here? What do you need from me?

- Do not argue or defend yourself. You are beginning a relationship. Just recognize that neither part of you may be comfortable yet. Don't be surprised or afraid if the Inner Critic is mean or angry at first. Just let it know you get whatever it is feeling. Be open and curious. Sometimes, the best thing is just to write, "Tell me more," and notice what happens. Do your best to come from your heart. If what you hear is upsetting, take a break (if you like) and come back later. Or, you can ask it not to be so scary. You can let it know how you are feeling, too. It *is* a two-way street. Come from your heart and not your head as best you can, and don't make promises you can't keep.

- Keep going for a while until you feel you have made a connection and are relating. Know that you have made an honest, sacred connection to a part of yourself that can serve you deeply and faithfully for the rest of your life. You can nourish this connection and see where it leads you.

By completing this exercise, my hope for you is that you will soon transform the voices that stop you.

And, if you're considering creating an online program, my best advice is to *make sure it suits you*.

You will spend a lot of time and energy creating, marketing, and selling your program, so make sure it engages you and fits your values. Make it fun! You *must* get joy from what you are doing. It needs to sustain you over the long haul.

Also, spend time figuring out who your ideal client is and what he/she is really looking for: not what *you* think is needed, but what that person tells you he/she needs. Then, devote yourself to serving that ideal client.

From there, do everything in your power to relate to your ideal clients authentically. Use *their* language. Not as a manipulation, but because you really get them, and because they have told you what they want. Keep refining the process.

Remember, the closer your ideal client is to you, the more successful you will be. You will ultimately be healing yourself, and who knows how to do that better than you?

* * *

 *Ahulani McAdam, founder of Shining Our Light on Earth, is a master psychic energy healer, artist, and spiritual mentor. She has been in practice with clients, leading groups and workshops in NYC, Europe, and California for almost forty years. She is passionate about supporting the emergence of the Feminine on Earth and women's empowerment. From suburban "good girl" to activist lawyer, adventurer, painter, and grandmother, her own life has been an embodiment of those goals. Ahulani is also the author of Conversations with Cancer: What Love Has to Do with It. She currently lives in Northern California and on Zoom! You can learn more about her here: shiningourlightonearth.com.*

Get Ahulani's free gift …

7 Kinds of Inner Critic and How to Transform Yours report to begin mastering your Inner Critic here:

TeachYourExpertiseBook.com/gifts

Chapter 9
Break the Fear
by Virginia Parsons

Before starting my visibility marketing business, I was a clinical hypnotherapist for many years. I attracted clients from many states to my "brick-and-mortar" office, and had built a good reputation for myself.

Of course, that kind of business came with its challenges. First, when a client wanted to see me in my office, it would require a time investment.

Many wanted to work with me remotely and asked if we could meet via phone sessions. I agreed to trying them, but wasn't very happy about not being able to see my clients, since much of my work depended on observing their response patterns.

I started looking for another way to meet virtually with clients. Video conferencing was in its infancy and very expensive. Then Skype came out with video calls, and I was excited to learn about the new technology.

Another challenge I came up against in my business was that my growth was limited by the one-on-one model. I wanted to find ways to leverage my time and work one-on-many.

The final blow to that business came during the 2009 recession. It became increasingly difficult to pay my operating expenses as the economy retracted. Plus, my aging mother needed more care, and I was the one to take most of it on.

I ultimately decided to close my office and work from my mother's home—a virtual business that would allow me to continue to work with people remotely while being there for her. Skype video calls proved to be less than stable, so the situation wasn't ideal … but I managed to make it work and still assist the few remaining clients I had retained.

It was in my continued exploration of other broadcasting options that I discovered Google Hangouts on Air, a robust system for streaming live. It was also rather technologically challenging to master. As my hypnotherapy practice waned, I spent more time mastering Hangouts.

I even started my first WebTV show, the *Savvy Shopper Show*, to help people find the best buys and specials online. I went on to own a shopping website with over 30-million products from well-known stores, which was a great way to get more visibility. I quickly discovered that livestreams got a lot of "Google SEO juice," and it was a perfect way to demonstrate some of my favorite products. This became my first venture into visibility marketing.

Soon, people began asking me to be their "Hangout Mentor" and teach them how to use the emerging technology. So, I started Hangout Marketing University, to teach people how to broadcast and present themselves professionally, so they could build their reputation as *the* "go-to expert" in their niche.

At the same time, the final blow was delivered to my hypnotherapy practice: the Nevada Psychological Association lobbied our legislature to ban the practice of hypnotherapy for anyone who was not a licensed psychologist. Despite hundreds of hours of certified trainings and over 20 years of clinical practice, I would no longer be able to charge for my services.

So, I changed course and started training people on how to broadcast on the new LIVE platforms. I specialized in Hangouts on Air at first, because that was the most powerful platform for going live at the time (Facebook LIVE did not even exist yet).

Then, I launched *The Inspirational Business Women Show* (now in its sixth season) and grew a loyal following on Google Plus.

Unfortunately, my business was totally focused on that platform. It was where my 10,000+ followers connected with me. When Google Plus shut down, leading to the later shut down of Hangouts on Air, my four-year old business had to be totally revamped.

BIG LESSON LEARNED: Never build a business around something you don't control.

I regrouped once again and started Media Spotlight Marketing in 2017 to meet the growing need of entrepreneurs and small business owners to get visible and SHINE online using livestream, video, and digital marketing.

And now, I am no longer dependent on one platform for my business success! I'm happy to be free of the overhead of a brick-and-mortar office and thrilled to work from home, where I support business owners from around the world with visibility marketing strategies to brand and grow their business.

For me, there is nothing more gratifying than seeing a business owner build an expert reputation using livestream and video marketing. Previously, these technologies were only available to businesses with a big budget. However, now, anyone willing to master these new (mostly free) technologies can reach a global audience and serve many more customers.

As more and more people started embracing live video and social media marketing, I observed a new problem unfolding. Entrepreneurs were starting to use livestream in their business, but the results were less than professional, and they were working hard to produce enough content.

How were they to balance the day-to-day requirements of running a business with the added pressure of creating compelling content for all the social platforms—content that positioned them as *the* expert in their niche?

It became apparent that most entrepreneurs needed to take a more systematic approach to content creation while reducing the overwhelm associated with social media marketing.

And I could help them with that!

I wanted to teach them how to produce and market ONE strategically planned LIVE Video and LEVERAGE it into over 20 pieces of compelling content that establishes their expertise and attracts more dream clients.

I had already (informally) developed a system for doing so in my *Inspirational Business Women Show*. I decided to use it to create a formal, step-by-step program, **Go LIVE! Leveraged**.

In addition to that system, I wanted to teach entrepreneurs how to offload both the content creation and distribution across multiple social platforms, so they could focus on running their business without social media overwhelm. Bottom line: They would learn how to produce one compelling live video each month to create all their social marketing content for the year. This was a lot less work and a lot more leveraged. (Thus, the name of the program.)

It was time to create the program. It wasn't easy, and I learned a LOT!

For example, one of the challenges in creating an online program was formalizing the intuitive process I had been using for my *Inspirational Business Women Show* into a systematic step-by-step program. But what I found was that the process was actually deeply rewarding, and in the end, I was able to bring to life what I had been doing for years without ever having realized I even *had* a system.

Now, I still had challenges to overcome … like my own resistance to creating another program. I had already developed several in my

Hangout Marketing University business, based on one livestreaming platform that no longer exists. It was imperative that any new program I created not be dependent on any one broadcasting platform. With Alina's encouragement and guidance, I decided that I had a unique skillset and knowledge base that could really help people. So, I took the plunge and developed my new online program, **Go LIVE! Leveraged**, so entrepreneurs could benefit from my many years of experience in planning and producing shows and live casts filled with inspiring, actionable content.

I also wanted the principles I taught to be universal and applicable to any livestream and social platforms to avoid the potential for outdated information. And that, right there, is probably the biggest lesson I learned: Do not develop an online course based on any one platform, technology, or program. If you do, you may have to continually update it or abandon it completely due to "extinction" as I had to. And that was a hard lesson!

Also, I quickly learned that "less is more" when developing an online program. Keep training videos short and to the point. Give bite-sized tasks so participants feel a sense of accomplishment with each concept taught.

I am still working on my tendency to overdeliver. Trust me, though, if a concept is not absolutely essential to participants getting the result they desire, leave it out.

I found it imperative to include LIVE mentoring in the program to provide extra support, so I implemented "Hug Seat" opportunities for mentoring. They can either be in group format or one-on-one, depending on your offer and price point. Recently, I added several LIVE Practice Labs, in which we work together on implementing tasks outlined in each module. Participants have really loved this added feature.

Finally, one more lesson worth sharing: I have found that providing a supportive, collaborative private group for members helps everyone feel more connected, accountable, and encouraged to "get it done" together.

There have been so many benefits to creating **Go LIVE! Leveraged**. It has enhanced my reputation as an expert in livestream and video marketing. It has further positioned me as someone who provides both one-on-one and online coaching around these strategies. I have also expanded the program into a Done-for-You Service called Interview Leveraged, where I interview my clients on a compelling topic that establishes their expertise and then provide all the content creation and leveraging for them. It's a "one-and-done" program for busy entrepreneurs who want to expand their reach without worrying about going LIVE on their own.

In other words, creating my online program has brought so many other opportunities my way.

One of the best "perks" is that I feel particularly rewarded by the leaps in confidence and visibility many of my clients in my program have experienced.

One participant started the program with NO experience in LIVE video. Now, she is running summits, interviewing dozens of leading experts, and totally comfortable and natural on camera. She is leveraging her interviews into multiple social marketing posts and is recognized as a true expert in her field!

Another client, who worked from home for many years, is a grandma who thought "technology" was a dirty word. However, she knew the importance of being visible online to grow her business. From feeling too timid to push the "Go LIVE" button to calling herself "the Livestream Queen," she has created over 800 videos which she simulcasts across five platforms. She knows exactly what to do, now as at home with technology as she is with her grandson. She has grown a six-figure business to support her retirement, and people love her video training.

I love getting these kinds of results for my clients! Watching their transformation is a beautiful thing ... especially because I know exactly what it's like to feel timid and afraid.

When I first started to explore using LIVE video in my business, I had all the usual fear and trepidation most people have. I had to overcome my fear of speaking on camera, as well as my fear of using an unfamiliar technology to go LIVE across the internet. I would get super nervous when I turned on the camera for a broadcast. My palms would sweat, my heart would race, and my mouth would get dry.

Maybe you can relate? Maybe, as you've read this chapter, your heartbeat accelerated even at the thought of going live in front of an audience?

I'd like to share with you how everything shifted for me.

I interviewed a female Navy Fighter Pilot who nearly lost her life in a plane crash.

It woke me up to real fear versus imagined fear.

You see, there is no death threat when going LIVE! Only perceived threat. Right? Will anyone watch? Will they like me? Will I make a fool of myself?

Although the fear of the camera is real, it can so easily be transformed into an excitement about connecting with people who are interested in your topic and what you have to say. THAT is truly transformative.

And that interview was my breakthrough.

If you feel a similar fear and hesitancy to go LIVE, here are some tips that may help you break through the fear just like the clients I shared with you above did.

Tip 1: Think of the camera as your friend. Look into the camera as though you are speaking to a good friend. The camera truly *is* your friend and your window to the world! It is the fastest path to build the "know, like, and trust factor."

Tip 2: Let go of "perfectionism." Be natural and authentic, and you will attract your ideal clients who resonate with your personality and passion.

Tip 3: Position your camera at eye level and look into it when speaking. This does take some practice, but is so worth it once you realize how much better you will connect with your audience. Many people with laptops tend to look down at the camera. Subconsciously, people feel like they are being looked down on when you broadcast this way.

Tip 4: If feeling timid, practice going LIVE privately at first. Broadcast to yourself! It's a great way to get over technology jitters.

Tip 5: Plan your content before you go LIVE, so what you share is compelling and helpful to the viewers. And of course, acknowledge your viewers and thank them for joining you. Get them engaged in the conversation by asking questions and probing for feedback.

And, if you are considering creating your own online course, on top of the tips I've offered throughout, here's my best advice. Just DO it!

People are waiting for the solution you provide. There is no better way to leverage your expertise and impact more people's lives than to create your own online program. More and more people are working from home and seeking training and education outside the traditional educational classroom. Your online program can become the foundation of your offerings and the perfect vehicle to leverage your expertise and knowledge!

* * *

Virginia Parsons is founder of Media Spotlight Marketing and Executive Producer of the Inspirational Business Women Show (now in its sixth season) and Media Spotlight TV (her newest endeavor). Virginia specializes in livestream, video and digital production, and video editing to help shine the spotlight on your business, so you can attract more clients in less time and get recognized as the market leader. To learn more about Virginia, visit MediaSpotlightMarketing.com.

Get 's Virginia's free gift ...

5 Easy Video Strategies Checklist to SHINE Online checklist and video training on the five best ways to use video strategies in your visibility marketing plan here:

TeachYourExpertiseBook.com/gifts

Chapter 10
The Roots of Body Transformation
by Allison Samon

I have always considered myself a health enthusiast. I enjoy working out in the gym, running, and lifting weights. I made an effort to eat "healthy." I strived to stay at my preferred weight and to fit well in my clothes—something I was always concerned about and actively "working on."

In retrospect, my vision of what it means to be "healthy" was superficial. The proof? While I was working on my muscle tone and flat abs so I could be beach ready anytime, I was also seeing neurologists for unexplained chronic pain.

It all started with a knee injury I suffered while skiing on college break. Then, I injured it again running a 5K the following summer. I went to my Primary Care Physician when it seemed to be taking an extra-long time to heal. He dismissed my concerns with a simple, "You're young. You're athletic. You're fine." Despite something inside of me insisting he was wrong, I took him at his word.

After a while, my other knee began to hurt, too, as a result of overcompensating for the injured knee and bearing all my weight. Eventually, it became so bad that co-workers had to carry me up and down the steep stairs at our television production studio in NYC. I felt like a little old lady at 24 years of age!

And it wasn't just my knees. I experienced a dull ache and numbness in my lower back and backside every time I sat, especially for long periods of time. Imagine, sitting to watch a movie, commuting to work, or even just to eat dinner, and having excruciating pain!

Living at home with my parents and commuting 40 minutes each way from New Jersey into Manhattan daily for my job on a popular soap opera, I was physically miserable. While at home, I blamed the patio furniture for not being ergonomic. I blamed the kitchen chairs. My mattress. At work, I was helping produce and direct a very sexy yet very demanding TV show, and the stress added to my discomfort. So, I was uncomfortable sitting, but when I got up to walk around to resolve that discomfort, my knees would swell! It was quite maddening, really, and it resulted in my cranky mood (all. of. the. time).

For someone my age, the pain itself—and the effects of that pain on my life—were extraordinary!

Worse, the pain kept manifesting, this time with the onset of migraines. My body warned me when they were coming with a taste of chlorine in my mouth and a funny sensation in my nose. Given the nature of my work, and the fact that I had my first migraine when I was 13 after my great grandmother's funeral, getting frequent migraines didn't seem all that surprising. Unfortunate, sure, but not surprising or uncommon. I was prescribed medication, and it was simply something I dealt with, as is often the case when it comes to recurring, and treatable, ailments.

I felt so old. I was so tired; I often fell asleep during movies. I even slept through a live performance of The Producers sitting in orchestra seats! I cried a lot. I couldn't make sense of why I felt so awful. The doctors were confounded and offered no solutions. For the better part of six years, I endured seven inconclusive MRIs. I saw neurologists, orthopedists, chiropractors, and physical therapists only to get the same recommendations to explore further with surgery, or keep continuing "treatment," which ranged from acupuncture (relieving one area but not the other) to physical therapy (a complete waste of time as I schlepped to make physical therapy appointments on time after work even though I saw zero improvement).

While on this seemingly endless quest, the unthinkable happened: my super-fit, fun-loving father suddenly died of heart disease no one knew he had. He was only 50 years old. Three months prior, he had gone for his annual checkup and colonoscopy. He was awarded a clean bill of health in March.

Yet on June 26, after playing tennis at a work event while entertaining clients, he died.

I was absolutely devastated on so many levels. He was my favorite person in the world and the one "ally" I felt I had in my nuclear family. And he was so young! Was the pain and struggle I was experiencing early warning signs? Taking a break from my treatments, I fell into a deep depression, feeling doomed to die young.

Eventually, I emerged from my cocoon and started seeing doctors again. I'm not sure where it came from, but I developed a renewed determination to get to the bottom of my pain. Perhaps it stemmed from feeling like I owed it to my dad to live *well*.

I changed the way I looked at my body; instead of seeing it as something that was dysfunctional and failing, I realized it was in need of support. What could *I* do to change the way it felt?

I saw every specialist anyone recommended, sure they were all missing something. Then, one miraculous day, I was introduced to a practitioner who thought outside the box. He was a health coach of sorts, and he illuminated for me a crazy new-fangled treatment you may have heard of …

Nutrition! I joke, but in all the years I spent seeing doctors, *not one* had ever asked me about what I ate. This practitioner showed me the connection between the things I put in my body and their effects on my health. He helped me discover nutrient deficiency, and how it all tied together with the other areas of my life, like the sleep issues, socializing, and self-care.

I took his wisdom and recommendations to heart, and very quickly, I re-gained feeling in my feet and backside. Next, I could walk up and down stairs again! I no longer needed medication for migraines and body pain. I lost the 10 pounds that forever fluctuated and kept them off for over 10 years now. Eventually, my co-workers began to notice the changes in me and wanted to know what I was on. (I promise you, caffeine and nicotine had nothing to do with it, ever). Previously, my "drug" of choice was sugar, but now, I no longer needed it to sustain my energy during long days!

It was the beginning of a radical transformation of my body *and* my life. And I couldn't help but wonder if a lack of nutrition was also responsible for my seemingly healthy dad dying so young.

Suddenly, I was hit with questions:

Am I meant to help people course correct after genetic warning signs, as I had? Is it possible that people don't have to suffer with chronic illness? Does our diet and lifestyle have a lot more to do with all of it than we're led to believe?

In 2011, I went back to school for nutrition and became a Certified Holistic Health Coach, and then, a Functional Nutrition and Lifestyle Practitioner. In 2014, I officially left the television and film business and opened Health Allie Lifestyle & Wellness.

My mission is to help busy people who are struggling with their weight, energy, and chronic illness to get fit, energized, and pain free in ways that are easy, fun, and sustainable.

It occurred to me that there were specific pearls of information I'd picked up along my years of struggling with my health and seeing so many diverse practitioners. What if I could cherry pick what worked for me, and offer it to others? My painful symptoms did not have official diagnoses, yet they resembled several autoimmune diseases. I was able to treat them, and reverse symptoms without the use of medications—how valuable it would be for me to help others struggling with pain do the same!

With that in mind, I created my coaching program, Healthy Without Struggle Blueprint. I designed it to teach people about their unique bio-individuality and help them to explore how it really feels in their body. This system then became the foundation for my first online program: **Sustainable Weight Loss for Crazy Busy Women**.

In essence, by teaching my clients how to recognize the signs and symptoms their own bodies express to them, I would teach them how to fish! I've been able to reach and support women who have suffered in silence for years.

For example, my client Jeana found me online after she'd seen a video I'd made sharing my story. We messaged back and forth, and then spoke on the phone before she decided to join my program. Boy, was she glad she did! Jeana hadn't been able to wear her wedding ring in two years, because her fingers were so swollen. In the morning, her hand would be so stiff, she would be unable to open it. She suffered with several autoimmune conditions that took turns flaring up and triggering each other, and she was 40 pounds overweight.

After taking my program, Jeana was able to not only open her hand, but use it to prepare food. This was huge in itself, as she was often too nauseated to eat. And even though she was now able to eat, she was also losing weight!

Within a month of our working together, she happy cried as she put her ring back on. She said, "*Sometimes, we just need a little direction, knowledge, and support to get there. Allie is AMAZING at what she does, and she does it with her whole heart. I already shared some of her recipes with my doctors, because they were so intrigued as to how I was getting better faster, and they wanted to know!! It's one day at a time, but you can do it. I love you, Allie, to the moon and back, and I look forward to working alongside you in the future to change lives.* "

Jeana is a perfect representation of my ideal client—someone with big health problems who has made big efforts to resolve them. Together, we "clear the muddy waters," as we say in functional nutrition, to uncover the root cause of the pain—which is virtually impossible to do with so much inflammation ("mud") clouding what we see.

And it works. I love hearing my clients report that, *"Finally, someone understands me and all I've been through, and still doesn't think I'm crazy! Finally, I feel energized and clear headed, and the weight is finally falling off. I haven't felt this good in years!"* (And I get that a lot!)

Because so many people suffer from a lack of nutrition or nutrient deficiency, I'm going to share just a bit more about the work I do, so you too can take the first steps toward feeling better!

First and foremost, I suggest removing the most inflammatory foods from your diet: gluten, dairy, refined sugar, and soy. Now, we don't want to get into a mentality of restriction or scarcity, which can then lead to binge eating, so it's important that we add in nourishing foods and track how they make you feel.

Tracking is non-negotiable, especially in the beginning. Keep a record—a Food – Mood – Poop Journal—of what you're eating, how you're eliminating (oh yes, we talk poop, pee, and gas on the daily!) and how you're feeling, including your mood. Also note any supplements or medications you may (or may not) take, hydration, and sleep. There is absolutely no judgement here—the point is to get some insight into what you are (and are not) doing, so we can look for patterns over time.

For example, if you are constipated after eating dairy several times a day/week, that is something to note and discuss. If you end each day with headaches, and your journal reflects a lack of water intake, that's a flag. If you suddenly feel the need to nap after lunch, we want to investigate why that might be.

The Food – Mood – Poop Journal, or FMP for short, will provide you with valuable insights into your day-to-day diet, and also help you note changes in your body.

Maybe you have an aversion to tracking your food, mood, and poop (it should be noted that the shape, color, and consistency of your bowel movements is very revealing when it comes to your health!). This exercise is an invitation to get curious about what's going on in your body. Tracking is a useful tool for illuminating signs, symptoms, and potential food sensitivities. Your brain is likely too focused on too many other things to accurately recall what you do and eat in a day. Making this effort for a relatively short amount of time will pay off in dividends in the end.

This is just the tip of the iceberg when it comes to what I teach in my program. And I love it, because it allows me to reach more women than I would otherwise be able to.

The beauty of creating an online program offered me the opportunity to work with over a dozen women with similar symptoms, yet different or no diagnoses, simultaneously. It provides them with the comfort of not feeling so alone in their suffering, too. It illuminated for me just how much confusion there is out there regarding nutrition and women's health, and how I could bring clarity and confidence not only to the women themselves, but also positively impact their spouses and children, as well.

I'll say this:

Building an online program can be a lot like deciphering your body's messages. I had to clear the clutter (in my brain) in order to make way for the program to come together in a coherent and cohesive way. The three biggest lessons I learned from my experience were:

1. I can build it as I go. It's unrealistic to expect the herculean task of creating content for a six-week program to happen in one day, or even one week (necessarily). It once felt insurmountable! But upon realizing that I really only needed an outline and ability to stay one week ahead of the program participants, it was like phew! What a relief! I tend to do things at the last minute anyway (or make changes up until showtime), so this was key for me. Had I not learned this, I'd likely still be caught up in analysis paralysis!

2. My audience does not know as much as I do, and they don't want to. I was determined to overdeliver, so I created SO MUCH content that I overwhelmed my group. Given that my program was geared toward crazy-busy women, I was basically reneging on my promise. I learned it's better to leave room for a next level program, and remember that people join a program for the results you promise—*not* to receive a professional education. They want to have a transformation, not just more information.

3. Have fun! I had actually tried to launch this exact program six months prior under a different name, working with a different team. Not only did I not have a rapport with the team of sub-contractors the person I hired had hired, but there was a mismatch creatively, as well. There was so much stress around the launch that it became an emotionally and financially miserable experience. After a full six-week launch, only two people bought (one was from my existing list, and the other, a referral!). This go around, I changed the title, shot a bunch of videos, and joyfully invited people to join the program as I was still working on it. I made changes based on conversations we had and the feedback I received. And it was a blast! I was making money and then doing the work, instead of spending money and what felt like begging people to sign up. If you're not having fun, customers will sense that energy, and they won't buy. But when you are, people want in!

And just like when your body begins to function optimally, your Entire Self starts to course correct—you and your body systems don't have to work as hard.

Creating an online program systematized how I run my business and leveraged my time. I no longer have to work as hard to attract and serve my clients, and I also get the space to be a new mom! My job is now to facilitate transformation for many people at once, instead of one person at many different times. There's an art and science to practicing Functional Nutrition, and I believe it is the future of healthcare.

★ ★ ★

Allison Samon (FNLP, CHHC)—aka Health Allie—is a Functional Nutrition and Lifestyle Practitioner and Certified Holistic Health Coach who specializes in demystifying complex health issues like weight loss and chronic pain to achieve sustainable results. She is a sought-after speaker and creator of several popular programs for women and men who are proactive and excited to take charge of their health. Allison believes that once people learn to recognize the signs their bodies are sending, they can get to the root cause, and avoid and even reverse disease, so they can live their best lives for themselves and their families. You can learn more about her here: www.allisonsamon.com.

Get Allison's free gift …

Food Sensitivity Diary to discover the why behind your symptoms and make adjustments that accelerate your journey toward optimal health and wellness here:

TeachYourExpertiseBook.com/gifts

Chapter 11
Science, Energy, and Spirituality ... Oh My!
by Christina Solstad

My parents, who were scientists and lovers of the natural world, instilled in me a deep curiosity about life. As a child, I was sensitive to the energies around me, and loved to escape into the edge of the woods across the street to commune with the trees and animals. When I was in high school, my mom took us to guided meditations, where I recall laying on the floor, eyes closed, as I was guided into a space that felt like home.

My curiosity and fascination with the magic of life (along with being the oldest child of scientists) led me to study science in college, learning transcendental meditation and embarking into a post-college career doing biomedical research in immunology at Harvard Medical School. From there, I worked for the Scripps Clinic and Research Foundation in La Jolla, California. Many years in the environmental field with a large corporation followed, working at the lab bench and in the field as a chemist, then leading a team ensuring compliance with (and negotiating environmental permits with) regulatory agencies.

Ultimately, though, I left corporate due to the stress and overall lack of humanity I experienced.

It was killing my soul.

My dad had survived a stress-induced heart attack a few years earlier, so when a spiritual teacher asked if I was going to have my "manager's heart attack" (while I was investing long hours doing all the work on a major project that my manager was taking the credit for), it struck me to my core, and I knew I needed to leave. The final straw came in the midst of some messy merger negotiations resulting in poor treatment of employees. I drummed up every bit of courage I had and went to talk with some high-level managers and VPs about what I saw versus the company line we were being told. When it was clear they weren't willing to change anything, acting as if they had no idea what I was talking about, I told my boss I was leaving, and why. Per company protocol, he was required to walk me out to my car, even though he understood.

I sat in my car and sobbed. What now?! I was leaving my work home of 15 years. Even though I never quite felt like I fit in that corporate environment, it was what I knew, and I was feeling the loss.

After the initial shock, I realized I actually now had a unique opportunity to do something *different*. But what? I thought about the reasons my colleagues and classmates would often come to me for help: writing reports, dealing with stress, or just for a safe place in which they could feel heard. Next, I considered my interests: meditation and spirituality, photography, writing, connecting with nature, travel, and exploring sacred places such as Chaco Culture National Historical Park in New Mexico, where I co-led week-long spiritual retreats with my teacher for several years, and have a site named after me (really!). I wrote a blog inspired by my connection to Chaco, called *Spirit of Chaco Blog: Deepening Your Connection to the Divine in the Sacred Sites of Chaco Canyon*.

I pursued copy editing to help my own writing, and ended up serving well over a hundred clients, mostly in the medical and environmental sciences. At the same time, energy healing intrigued me enough to become a Reiki Master and teach others Reiki.

While taking a course on the energy of prosperity, I heard the instructor coach another participant, and something deep within me stirred. I immediately knew I wanted to learn how to do what he did! When they offered a 10-month training and certification for energy coaching, I had a deep intuitive "Yes." I had never invested that much money in myself before, and had no conscious idea of what was to come.

Still, my heart and spirit knew it was my path.

As with many of the trainings and certifications I underwent, I was motivated first by the benefit to myself—helping others transform their lives brings me true joy and fulfillment. I found my calling as a coach and healer, even as the particulars have continued to shift over the years.

In 2012, I started The Financially Free Woman, my energy coaching business. Since then, it has expanded (as I did, earning several certifications along the way and combining them with my intuitive knowledge and experience) into the energy and spirituality of money and abundance, more powerful energy tools, and intuitive business coaching with an emphasis on clearing the barriers standing in our way, and opening the flow to move forward, create true abundance, and reconnect with and share the brilliance within ourselves.

Because the truth is, the world *needs* our gifts *now*. That is why we are here!

Underlying the work I do with my clients is a deep spirituality that is grounded in science. I call it "practical spirituality." It is who I am, and what I get to bring to my clients. I have always served as a bridge between the often-disparate worlds of spirituality and science, seeing both as needed and connected. I get so excited as science continues to validate spiritual and energetic concepts we have known for eons, and the discussion has become more mainstream. As this bridge, I see connections (or options) my clients may miss, that are perhaps not quite so apparent at first.

As my business evolved, I found I was having trouble encapsulating and describing what I do for clients, making it difficult to market and grow my business effectively.

Creating an online program to grow my business was at first only a vague consideration—*maybe once I develop some of my own methods, and become more confident,* I thought. I wasn't there yet. When colleagues asked if I would consider creating a program, my answer was always no; after all, what would it be about? I didn't want to just recreate what someone else had already done. Besides, I had no idea where to begin. It seemed like a monumental undertaking.

Finally, I decided to attend Alina Vincent's event on creating programs, mostly because she was a friend and colleague, and I wanted to support her. I was also curious. Even then, just in thinking about it, I struggled to come up with a program topic and content; *maybe it could be something around money and abundance,* I contemplated.

The day after the event, everything seemed to "magically" come together. While relaxing and discussing ideas with a colleague, I realized I had been overthinking it (the analytical scientific part of me, right?). Once I stopped thinking so hard about doing it the "right way," or finding the "perfect idea," or thinking I didn't know enough, and tuned into what I intuitively knew and was already helping clients with, the ideas bubbled up.

My **Unlock Your Money Mojo** online program was born! It felt right. And it was my creation, not anyone else's methods or system!

I launched the program in late 2018, filled it with eager participants, and witnessed them experience transformations in how they viewed and approached money again and again. They expanded how much they were willing to ask for and receive. They released inner blocks and beliefs that had been in their way of creating and keeping more money, and created new empowering beliefs. And they felt more confidence, more joy, and more lightness around money and abundance (and in their life).

Not only that, but creating a program helped me to step more fully into my power and own my expertise, because I had something tangible to offer people—something concrete I could point to and speak about—that incorporated all my own energetic work, knowledge, intuition, and methods of doing things.

It provided me with a focus for my work and marketing, and allowed me to leverage my time and expertise while growing my business.

As an added bonus, I discovered that I *love* the energy of the live group calls I hold as part of the program, too! Folks participate fully, and not only interact with and learn from me, but also with and from each other. Strong bonds are created, and it's a total win-win! This is a super-valuable part of the program, as the group feature has benefits not available in the same powerful way in one-on-one coaching.

Here's what one of my program participants, Nurjahan, said about her experience in Unlock Your Money Mojo:

"I experienced so many openings when I joined Christina's Unlock Your Money Mojo program. Just in the first week alone, I ended up bringing in five times the original offer on a gig. I uncovered so many blocks—some that I didn't even realize I had around money! The program was so thorough. She literally walked us through every step. I'm so grateful for all of the ways her program has helped me, my family, and my business!"

Kinga had a powerful breakthrough, too:

"This was a very powerful program for me. One of my major breakthroughs was how my money story related to relationships. In a past relationship, I had started believing I did not know how to take care of money because he controlled it—so I avoided money altogether. I ran away from it. Thanks to the program, I learned how to take back my power. I can be responsible for my money. That was a major breakthrough for me."

I also love how my online program provides me with a bigger reach. After all, so many of us struggle at one point or another with money!

Right now, I'd love to share with you one of my favorite exercises from my program, to help you take the first steps toward accessing *your* money mojo!

The "What Is Your Relationship with Money?" Exercise

Sit comfortably and imagine the following scenario:

You are sitting on a bench, and someone sits down next to you. You immediately turn away from him or her. Ignoring the person, you say out loud:

"You are so dirty and greedy. You are bad. I don't like you. Go away!"

How long do you think that person would stay beside you? Right … not long at all!

Money is no different.

Monitor your thoughts. Are you ignoring, or speaking badly about money, but then wondering why you don't have more? Are you pushing it away because of your hidden (or not-so-hidden) inner dialogue (*"I can't be spiritual and have money"*; *"I have to work super hard for money"*)?

What sort of relationship would you love to have with money instead? What if you thought of money as a person—a best friend or lover? How would you treat it then? What would you say to it?

Journal your thoughts and insights. Then, have some fun experimenting with new ways to treat and talk to money. Be outrageous. Switch things up. Then, watch the magic happen!

Finally, if you are considering creating a program, here's my advice:

Do it!

Not only does it have the potential to expand your business, but you'll grow as a person and entrepreneur, too.

Three of the biggest lessons I learned from creating my Unlock Your Money Mojo program are:

- I have something valuable to offer people.

- I don't need to do things the way others do. (One of my clients told me no one else teaches money and abundance the way I do, and that is why she loves it!)

- Trust myself, my experience, and my wisdom, and what comes through me intuitively.

Don't let your doubts stop you!

Yes, even if you think, like I did, that you don't have anything to create a program about, or that you are "not there yet." You may be surprised how much you do know, and how valuable that knowledge is to others. Remember, there are those who need and are looking for your expertise, even if it seems like it is too simple. You may think, *"Doesn't everyone know this?"* No, they don't. That is why they need you and your program!

Christina Solstad is the creator of Unlock Your Money Mojo, a spiritual program for entrepreneurs who want to create radical shifts in their relationship with money. After working for years as a scientist, including at Harvard Medical School, Christina brings a grounded approach to her spiritual work. Her clients

range from brand-new business owners who want to make more money to wildly successful entrepreneurs who struggle to keep and grow their cash flow. Her client roster includes Fortune 5000 companies, brick-and-mortar businesses, entrepreneurs, coaches, healers, and more. When she's not helping her clients create true abundance, you can find Christina taking a long stroll down the beach or planning her next adventure to Chaco Canyon, Africa, Egypt, Nepal, New Zealand, Australia ... wherever her heart calls her. You can learn more about Christina here: www. TheFinanciallyFreeWoman.com.

Get Christina's free gift ...

Money Manifesting Mantras to quickly increase the flow of money and abundance to you here:

TeachYourExpertiseBook.com/gifts

Chapter 12
Tapping into Healing
by Jan Luther

If you knew you could shift your mood and attitude and heal past trauma and grief in as little as 20 minutes, would you be interested?

The sixth of seven children born into a very German family in a rural town in Idaho, I grew up with a lot of stress. I witnessed alcoholism and rage daily. By the time I was in my early 20s, I had experienced so much trauma and fear that I am certain I was suffering from what we now refer to as ACE (Adverse Childhood Experiences).

All the anger and abuse taught me to be hypervigilant at all times. That stress had a profound effect on me physically and mentally: it damaged my nervous system and created a fear-based mindset. Even in my happiest moments, I struggled deeply with self-loathing, lack of trust, and anxiety. This of course led to unrelenting emotional and physical pain.

I suffered from regular migraines, nearly constant back pain, and was at one time even hospitalized for depression.

Later, as the wife of a US Submariner, the change and pressure of being a 'single' parent while my husband was out at sea six to nine months at a time aggravated my anxiety and social phobias. I remember having to literally force myself to leave the house some days.

Add to that the traumas of moving every 18 months or so with four little children in tow, and it is no surprise that the depression was ever-deepening.

I continued to "white knuckle" my way through life.

My husband retired from the Navy in 1997 after 20 honorable years of service. We left the Navy with no jobs, no home, and no clear future vision for our little family. It was terrifying.

Six months later, my mother died. The weight of that loss on top of the quicksand of unknowns in our new life felt like the absolute most pain I could endure.

And then, in the summer of 2000, I was introduced to this bizarre concept called "tapping." I confess that I scoffed at the prospective benefits. But I was desperate, and since doctors only offered prescription medication, I was willing to put my pride aside and try anything.

Within minutes of trying it out, I felt instant and undeniable relief!

My mind was calmer, my nervous system "down-shifted," and my distress level was the lowest it had ever been!

Needless to say, I had to learn more.

Throwing myself into tapping, I proceeded to heal a lifetime of traumas, shame, grief, and depression within one year! For the first time in my life, I was able to think clearly when confronted with negative emotions. I could sort out the B.S. stories my mind was telling me and find my center and calm in any given moment.

Over time, the emotional and physical healing led to my tapping into a wealth of intuition, gifts, and talents that humble and surprise me to this day.

I opened my tapping business, The Rejuvenation Station, LLC in 2001 to help others experience the same remarkable healing I was enjoying.

Soon, many of my students began expressing interest in training and mentoring around starting their own EFT practice, and I was happy to help.

In 2004, Gary Craig, the creator of EFT Tapping, held the first EFT Masters training, and I was honored to be among the candidates. I received the title of EFT Master and was certain I had found my ultimate purpose and path in life.

And then …

You knew it was coming, right?

In August 2006, our 22-year-old son died in a car accident, and everything I thought I knew about my life, purpose, and identity fell apart.

Without tapping and the many grief processes I'd developed over the years prior to his death, it's highly unlikely that I would have lived to speak about the loss of my son.

It took a lot of time, but eventually, I was able to emerge on the other side of this tragedy with a renewed passion for sharing the healing tools that saved me with the millions of people who suffer from depression, anxiety, grief, and trauma every day.

To do that effectively, it became crystal clear to me that I needed to pivot from my one-on-one private coaching business model to online programs.

In my search for a mentor to help me do so, I found Alina and her High Profit Programs live event. I was so excited! She was doing exactly what I wanted to do: offering mastermind groups, live events, and group coaching from her brilliant pre-recorded and consistently updated online content.

Hallelujah!

Now, I'll be honest; I had to work through some doubts and fears about this transition.

First, I was worried that since Alina was primarily teaching business skills, the aspects of my trainings that are intended to *hone your intuition and tune you into quantum healing energy* wouldn't translate in an online course.

Second, I'm an empath. My ideal clients are heart-centered female business owners who are intuitive, too. The story in my head was that they wouldn't feel seen and supported with pre-recorded videos. I thought they needed to be with me in person.

And finally, I was afraid my people wouldn't complete the program on their own.

Using tapping and intuition, I began to challenge all those fears, and I quickly came to realize some wonderful truths:

Energy is not limited by time or space. The love and support I offer in a live class transfers beautifully in video. To my delight, many of the participants in my online program, **The EGO Tamer(R) Tapping Mentoring for Certification and Business Building**, told me they were just as entranced watching me on video!

Plus, my empathic students are almost always introverts. These beautiful, sensitive souls often consider the privacy and quiet of their own home or office as the perfect setting for their learning—they are more relaxed, centered, and open to their own wisdom than they would be in a live training.

And finally, fearing they wouldn't complete the program has proven to be totally unfounded. The hosting platform we use allows me to easily track every student's progress step by step. They mark each lesson complete, so they get the thrill of seeing their progress, and I can ensure that no one falls through the cracks or gets left behind.

Here is just a bit of the feedback I've received from students:

"Thank you for putting the time and effort into making these {training videos}. I feel like I have you all to myself!"

"You always have such deeply inspiring insights. It's wonderful that I can pause the recording and take my time to savor your beautiful words."

"I feel like I have all the time in the world. I can pause a recording for whatever reason, and then, when I feel ready to start again, I push play, and there you are, waiting patiently for me. This healing is so deep, girl!"

Yup, a single tear is rolling down my cheek as I type.

Plus, with 90% of the required teaching and training materials pre-recorded, I have the time, freedom, and energy to fully engage with my students through our Facebook group and on our monthly calls.

Not only have my major fears been alleviated, but my conversion rate speaks volumes to the effectiveness of my new business model:

100% of the students who were sincerely interested in starting a business registered for my yearlong mentorship for certification after the TET Tapping training this year!

Maybe right now you're thinking this sounds amazing, but . . .

The voice in your head is protesting:

"It sure sounds like a lot of work. I've never done anything like this before. Can I really do it?"

"Can online trainings really convey the value of my teachings?"

"How can I be absolutely sure that the content I offer online is providing everything that is really needed to my students?"

I get it!

And my answer to all those questions is a hard "yes."

First, yes, you CAN really do it! You probably already have a couple of mini-programs in place in your current business.

For example, if you're a coach, do you have a client intake form?

Do you recreate that form for every new client you work with? Or have you created a standardized set of questions each client answers?

If you do have that one form, do you also have a system to automate its delivery to the prospect?

And once they have completed said form, do they have the ability to automatically submit it directly to your inbox?

It's *all* automated, right?

While rudimentary, your intake form and scheduling process are basically mini-versions of an online program. Easier for you—easier for your client. Everybody benefits!

An online program is the same concept, and the benefits to you and your clients are innumerable.

It can provide you with:

- Guaranteed monthly income. (Isn't it time you took some vacation?)

- The ability to increase your income whenever you need or want.

- Confidence in making your impact, creating a legacy, and essentially, a dreamy retirement plan.

- A greater reach and impact. Anyone, from all walks of life and anywhere in the world, can participate at any time, on his/her time. (Student can literally heal, learn, and grow while you sleep or take a vacation!)

- Ease of delivery. An online program allows you to clear virtually every hurdle associated with delivering your content live. And you get to keep the brilliance you're sharing simple, palatable, and fun.

- Freedom! It's like having a team of employees who work all day, every day, no holidays or vacation days needed, for free!

And, because your content will naturally and incrementally build as your students' skills and proficiency grows, they naturally generate their own excitement and momentum, which is so rewarding for them and for you!

Win-win and score!

Still feeling a little hesitant?

I'd love for you to do an experiment with me right now to give you a taste of the work I do.

The Boomerang Game:

Start by reading the phrase below out loud, and then, quickly quiet your mind to observe the immediate echo from your subconscious EGO mind.

Ready?

"I'm so thrilled to have an online program up and running with (dozens/hundreds) of students (or clients) paying me (hundreds/thousands) of dollars each and every month!"

Shhhh ... listen ... what do you observe?

Is there any form of resistance, fear, and/or tension in your body?

Obviously, this affirmation isn't true in the present moment (since you're likely reading this to start building your online program), so let's honor that layer of resistance.

Consider the bigger question: how hopeful or fearful did it make you feel to think about creating an online program?

On a scale of 0 to 10, with 10 being really resistant, afraid, overwhelmed, or even angry, how high would you rate your mental and emotional resistance?

Note: You can use this game any time you want to figure out why you are stuck in any way. Simply state the positive you are hoping for and LISTEN for the echo of EGO's fear and false belief.

Now, let's experiment with softening that resistance.

Experiment: Tapping Away Resistance

If you're familiar with tapping, awesome! Tap along and speak the words out loud S L O W L Y!

If you've never heard of tapping, not to worry. It cannot hurt you in any way, and often times, the shift is so undeniable that you feel nearly instant relief! (If you'd like to view my tapping points video for further direction, visit my website listed below, and scroll to the bottom to "Quick Links.")

Karate Chop:

Even though I may have some hesitation about creating an online program, I deeply and completely acknowledge that, right here, right now, no one is expecting me to. (Take a breath.)

Karate Chop:

Even though there's a part of me that may LOVE the idea, there may be another part that does not like it at all. For whatever reason, it may feel (use some of your own words) too much, too hard, too foreign, or too impossible.

I deeply and sincerely appreciate that all of these fears are a reflection of my values. This is, in part, my way of wanting to do things "right." (Take a breath.)

Karate Chop:

Even though it's possible that my mind is judging, condemning, and blocking me from trying this new thing …

… I like knowing that it's merely watching out for me. It's trying to keep me from being hurt. Disappointed. Failing. Embarrassed.

I'm open to recognizing that by blocking me, for any reason, this part of my mind is actually keeping me FROM trying something that may be awesome and amazing!

Top of Head:

Open to the idea of simply observing these fearful thoughts and feelings.

Between the Eyes:

Quieting and balancing my heart, mind, and body.

Side of the Eyes:

Allowing my energy to slow . . . slow . . . slow . . . down.

Under the Eyes:

Recognizing that, if my mind or energy is spinning, I cannot feel at ease.

Under the Nose:

Thanking my mind for watching out for me and my safety.

Chin:

Opening my heart and mind to allow for Divine Inspiration and Guidance, in whatever form I'm comfortable with.

Collarbones:

If I have read this far in the book, some part of me is curious.

Interested? Eager? Intrigued? I'm choosing to remain open to the idea of entertaining and nurturing the part of me that would love to serve more people . . . with less effort . . . and greater prosperity for all.

Under the Arm:

Acknowledging that resistance unchecked becomes failure.

Ribs:

The only way I'd truly fail, is if I don't even try.

(Take a deep breath.)

Next Round:

Karate Chop:

Even though I realize I probably don't have enough information or support yet to make a truly educated decision . . . I deeply and sincerely like the idea that this is me, trying on an idea—doing my due diligence and listening to dozens of others who have tried and succeeded at the very thing I am interested in.

Relaxing and releasing tension and concerns.

I am safe.

(Deep breath.)

Karate Chop:

Even though, I probably . . . maybe . . . definitely want to have a successful business (can you hear me giggling?), I want to make a huge impact for good in the world.

I love the idea of (use the word that best describes your product or service) helping, healing, coaching, nurturing, serving others.

Wouldn't it be fantastic, if I could multiply myself and help dozens, hundreds, maybe even thousands more people, every single day, without adding one hour's work to my schedule??

(INHALE and slowly exhale.)

Karate Chop:

Even though I'm sure I've tried new things before, who hasn't? And while some of them turned out less than fabulous, I know some have been very fulfilling.

I'm recognizing today, that as a person/coach/healer, I intuitively know there is much more for me to learn, do, and experience in this lifetime.

I don't have to do it all.

I don't have to do it all this year.

I just want to discern if the idea of an online program would benefit me, my clients, and my dreams and goals soon.

Top of Head:

One day at a time.

Between the Eyes:

One task at a time.

Side of the Eyes:

Maybe I will. Maybe I won't. I'm asking my Intuition to speak to me from my heart now.

Under the Eyes:

I'm open to feeling excitement as an intuitive "yes."

Under the Nose:

Or, open to feeling an intuitive "no." And I will simply say, thank you.

Chin:

I love knowing that the choice is and always will be mine to make!

Collarbones:

Releasing sadness, pain, and grief from any past disappointments. I don't have to do this alone.

Under the Arm:

Inviting my inner wisdom to lead and guide me.

Ribs:

Grateful to know. My business IS my business.

What would I like to do next?

Take a couple of slow, deliberate breaths.

***

How are you feeling?

Did you notice deeper breathing?

Even if the words aren't exactly yours, the tapping has a potent healing effect on your fight, flight, freeze response.

Let's retest your distress and resistance. Do you remember your number from before?

Now, on a scale of 0 to 10, with 10 being really resistant, afraid, overwhelmed, or even angry, how high would you rate your mental and emotional resistance to creating an online program?

Did the number go down?

Don't be discouraged if it didn't plummet. Any reduction is proof you've reduced your inner tension and unhealthy negative emotions.

Hopefully, your number reduced by three or more, and if so, congratulations!

You have now witnessed for yourself that *you have the power to heal your life literally at your fingertips!*

So, my dear. What's next for you? Are you ready to begin creating your online program?

I can sincerely say that doing so was one of the best steps I've ever taken in building my business over the past 20 years.

I hope that, whatever you choose, your life and business become everything you dream them to be.

* * *

Jan Luther has been practicing heart-centered healing and coaching for nearly 20 years. She's worked with experts, authors, healers, and coaches around the world. One of only nine US Founding EFT Master Practitioners, she's also the creator of The EGO Tamer® Tapping and Healing Your Grief programs. She is the author of Grief Is . . . Mourning Sickness and co-author of Mastering the Art of Success with Jack Canfield. You can learn more about her here: janluther.com.

Get Jan's free gift …

Erase Your Resistance to Marketing Your Business mini-program to discover the foundation for shifting mindset and emotions using TET Tapping here:

TeachYourExpertiseBook.com/gifts

Chapter 13
Sharing the Vision of What's Possible
by Emma Auriemma-McKay

My discovery of artist, architect, and engineer Leonardo DaVinci when I was 16 set the trajectory for my life.

I admired him as an artist, architect, inventor, and visionary. Excelling in all arts and envisioning beyond the normal scope of reality in his time, he was the ultimate Renaissance man—the Steve Jobs of his time. I wanted to follow in Leonardo's footsteps as the 21st Century Renaissance Woman!

I had building in my DNA; I was on a job site before I was born. My grandfather was building our family home at that time, and my mother would keep an eye on the progress during the end of her pregnancy. A few of my uncles were in the building trades, so I was often around fresh concrete and newly sawed wood in my early days. I still cherish those wonderful aromas!

When I was 12, I entertained myself by drawing house plans. My favorite one was an octagonal house with an open courtyard in the center.

I also had artistic talent. In second grade, I drew a barn with animals behind folded doors and a piggy with a curly pipe cleaner tail for my ill aunt. I brought it in to school for show and tell, and my teacher was so impressed, she brought me around to the other classrooms to show it off. I loved to do portraits, too, and when I saw Leonardo's Mona Lisa, I was totally wowed!

I followed in Leonardo's footsteps: I studied and went on to become an architect, which involves envisioning with an artistic eye, and creating "livable" art, so to speak. Eventually, I also became an artist, because it was something I was *compelled* to do. When I paint, I get into a zone, and the work is basically channeled through me.

I mostly paint landscapes. It takes a great deal of observation and study to capture the essence of a scene, and it has to be done quickly. When painting plein air (outdoors), light is a key factor, and there is only a window of a couple of hours to capture the same shadows, light quality, and colors (usually early or late in the day). Painting plein air is very experiential—you are in the elements, and you feel them, whether it's hot, cold or windy. Every painting I have ever done holds a story about the experience, along with a powerful "feeling and memory sensation of the situation." If it's an abstract, it's an evaluation of each step of the process to ensure the colors are coordinated, the space and depth are defined, and the composition makes it "feel" right.

This ties in with my architectural work. I design spaces to "feel right" … actually, to feel wonderful, so that it becomes a haven for the body, mind, and soul to enjoy. I tend to incorporate each of my experiences: from my travels, reading, or in keeping pace with the design industry. Practicing architecture involves being sensitive to and aware of the environment in which the design exists and the way the structure will be used and enjoyed by the occupants.

Being an architect is amazing! We're creatives, inventors, innovators, problem solvers, and visionaries. We use a part of our brain most people don't have access to. We can envision and virtually experience the three-dimensional, finished product based on a two-dimensional floor plan. It's like putting a puzzle together. We manipulate and mold the space our clients have to work with by incorporating their living requirements with our expertise and creativity to design a home or building that functions perfectly for them—and looks beautiful.

As you may or may not realize, our environment has an enormous impact on our lives, emotions, and sense of well-being. We spend about 90 percent of our lives indoors, and about 75 percent of our lives in our homes. So, it only makes sense that all of us should live and work in environments that serve us and make us feel good.

Throughout my 25-year career, I've often noticed how people are generally unaware of how their spaces can function and feel better. In many cases, they simply accept and live with what they have.

And, when clients *did* come to me for a remodel, they were often unfamiliar with and anxious about the process, because they didn't know what to expect. I started writing questions to help them prepare for our initial meeting and to give them time to think and understand what they wanted and needed. This gave me a clear direction how to help them right from the start.

Over time, I realized that preliminary client guidance was lacking—an explanation of the process from concept and budget to construction for the actual remodel.

In the early days of my practice, I saw many clients struggle with the process. Many of them had sticker shock when the contractor bids came in. Then, as the project went on, they felt out of the loop because they didn't understand the process or the lingo, or realize the level of their own involvement that the whole project required.

These elements—exploration, designing, and building—are standard across the board in the architecture/building industry no matter which state the project is in. However, members of the general public have little familiarity with it unless they have gone through a building project before. And even then, they may not have had proper guidance and education.

Another dynamic I noticed: many homeowners bought houses they planned to remodel or update, but they (and their real estate agents) couldn't always envision the great possibilities, or what a remodel/update project might entail.

So, I created my company, **Stress-Free Remodeling**, to give clients the information and guidance they need throughout the entire process.

Then, I realized real estate agents could benefit from similar information I'd been sharing with homeowners! They could use my process to envision what was possible with a property, sell homes faster, and, potentially, increase a home's value. It was exciting to discover how my architectural skills could be applied to an entirely different industry. (I encourage you to brainstorm how your skills can be used in another industry, as well.)

I had so much important information to share—information that could change the lives of homeowners and real estate agents!

From the questions I developed for my initial client meeting, the idea for a program began to percolate in my mind. I stumbled around for a few years with the idea because I didn't have direction or structure.

In 2017, I began working with my amazing coach, Alina Vincent. After our first Rising Stars Mastermind meeting, I told her I wished I'd hired a coach years ago! She helped me position myself as an expert and develop new resources to help my clients on a deeper level. With her structure, process, and guidance, I created my online program *in just three months*!

As I mentioned, people who are planning a build or remodel are often first timers, and they aren't clear on what the process involves and requires. They are apprehensive and don't know where to start.

The Ultimate Stress-Free Remodeling Blueprint is meant to act as a partner throughout the process, 24/7. It's like having an architect on hand around the clock. This guide gets property owners ready to work with their architect and helps them avoid costly mistakes.

Being prepared for their remodel will reduce their stress, so they can enjoy the process as their ideas come to life.

For real estate agents, it's a perfect intake system: it helps them get clear on how their clients may use their houses, in tangible ways, and which intangible elements are important to them. It also helps them find hidden value in a property, so they can envision the possibilities and share those with their clients who are selling or buying a property.

That was a basis for creating a second program specifically designed for real estate agents. It has a slightly different focus, but it includes all the valuable information that is most useful for them.

Alina, an intuitive coach, did for me what I do for my clients. She envisioned how my business could grow. She saw the potential in me and my business, and by pushing my envelope and expanding my horizons, she guided me to bring to life a much larger vision than I'd ever imagined.

That experience in itself showed the incredible value of working with a coach. It helped me see and understand the value I have to my clients—I can help them transform their lives! In fact, Alina suggested focusing on real estate agents since they could use the Ultimate Stress-Free Remodeling Blueprint not only for their own business strategies, but also as affiliate partners—they can offer it to their clients, which positions them as a great resource.

Working strictly as an architect, I am limited to a total architectural project only in the states where I'm licensed: California and Nevada. However, people from all over the world can take advantage of the educational elements I've added via the Ultimate Stress-Free Blueprint!

When I originally thought about creating a program, I imagined it as the fulfillment of an *ultimate* goal—to help more people than I could through my direct architect-to-client role to have a successful and enjoyable remodeling experience. That at the time that was my end goal and I didn't think about anything beyond that.

But here's what surprised me: creating this program was just the beginning. It unleashed a whole spectrum of opportunities, as well as a set of skills and activities I didn't even realize I'd enjoy. It empowered me in an even broader spectrum of ways.

With the new focus and direction I uncovered during my work with Alina, I had a springboard for other products and services which I'd never even considered creating or doing. Now, I'm an author and speaker, and the host of two podcasts … and who knows what else will come up?

I wrote my number one best-selling book, *The Homeowner's Guide to Stress-Free Remodeling*, and launched my podcast, *Stress-Free Remodeling*. The book and podcast led to invitations to speak in person and on other podcasts—which wouldn't have happened if I hadn't gotten so clear on my core message and had such a unique product to offer people.

And, because I have created resources that help real estate agents as well as homeowners, I have a national network of professional support, which helps me grow my business and brings extra value to my clients to serve them to the highest good. Also, learning online marketing strategies affords me a global network of people to help sell my programs, far from the traditional word-of-mouth method I used for my architectural practice.

I know what I've created actually works. For example, my client Karen was already building her new home when she came across the Ultimate Stress-Free Remodeling Blueprint. While some of the information in the program reassured her that she was doing some things right, other information brought to her attention some of the things she'd overlooked. Overall, she felt better equipped to navigate the home-building process after she reviewed my program.

Maybe, like Karen, you'd also love to transform a space where you spend a lot of time.

I'd like to walk you through an exercise right now to get started.

Ready?

Sit in your favorite place in your home. Take a few minutes to just *BE* in that space. Breathe deeply, and let your thoughts go.

Once you've relaxed, take some time, look around to really evaluate why you enjoy it... why it feels good to you ... why it's your favorite place.

Consider things like the light quality or the view from the window. Do you like the spacious feeling created by a high ceiling, or the coziness created by a low ceiling? What about the textures on the wall? The paint colors?

If your other rooms don't give you this type of good feeling, consider what's missing, based on what you enjoy about your favorite place. Use those qualities to enhance the other rooms in your home, so they make you feel just as good.

I sincerely hope these tips help you create spaces where you feel good; seeing people love their homes brings me joy!

This exercise is an example of the type of information I include in my programs to help transform lives by creating a space that enhances a person's daily existence. The beauty of an online program is that it can provide a transformation in *any* aspect of our lives, such as business, relationships, and personal development.

Which brings me to my *favorite* thing about programs: they empower us, as business owners, to share our gifts and expertise with, and facilitate a transformation for, more people than a one-on-one business model does. In fact, building a program has myriad benefits for *any* business.

Creating a program is a unique opportunity to use your skills, talents, gifts, and knowledge to help others, as I have done, and also to build your business—possibly even in ways you never imagined.

The result: you serve an even greater number of people, and you discover even greater opportunities.

Here are five steps I recommend if you are ready to get started creating your first program:

Step 1. First, identify your skills. What do you do best? Which of your skills is most transformational for other people? Or, which could you apply to another industry, like I did? In my case, my number one skill is envisioning a finished project. I'm naturally skilled at helping homeowners walk through the process to make their vision reality. I did it without realizing it was such an important skill! This may be the case for you, too. Sometimes, we don't even recognize our best skills because they come so naturally to us. If you're having a hard time dialing in on yours, ask some of the people you've worked with.

Step 2. Next, identify your ideal client. Be specific. In my case, I originally worked with homeowners who were planning a remodel project. Later, I realized real estate agents could benefit from the information I was sharing since they often helped homeowners buy properties that they planned to remodel or update.

Step 3. Then, identify five steps that are key to taking your client through their transformation. While there may actually be 15 steps to get them there, when it comes to an online program format, five steps (or modules) seems to be the sweet spot. If you know there are more, you may have content for additional online programs (think Level 1, 2, and 3).

Step 4. Create your program: break down each of the five steps you identified, then expand on each. Include stories proving your process.

Step 5. Get it out there! Use your network to share your program with the world. Look for unique ways to market, too. For example, I learned that I could leverage associations and professional organizations to do the marketing for me! By getting my real estate agent program approved for continuing education credits in Nevada (and soon, other states), the real estate agents' professional organization promotes it to their entire association.

An important note: While creating your program is a primary goal, and it may feel like THE way to expand your reach, help more people, and grow your business, be open. You may be surprised to find it can actually serve as the launching point for creating an even larger impact, like it did for me. You take one leap and realize if you take another one it will take you to an even more interesting place!

It can be the beginning of many great opportunities to come (for me, it was speaking, writing a book, and launching a podcast, among other things).

Since I launched my online programs, I've experienced increased credibility, more opportunities, and more professional fulfillment as I've discovered latent talents I previously hadn't accessed.

As I look back on the past several years, I realize I've accomplished an enormous amount. I'm so excited about the new directions I'm going, the new resources I've created, and the amazing people I have met and who have supported me along the way. Creating a program can do the same for you. Your professional skills can expand your business … and you never know where one program can lead you: it can grow your business *and* you as a person, so you can live an amazing life.

* * *

Emma Auriemma-McKay is a licensed NCARB Architect, a certified NCIDQ Interior Designer, and a LEED certified professional. She began her 25-year career working for international firms and big-name clients, which gave her the opportunity to be involved in a wide variety of projects, from high-rise commercial buildings to five-star luxury hotels such as the Mandalay Bay and Four Seasons in Las Vegas, the Hilton Hawaiian Village in Honolulu, and the Pan Pacific Convention Center in Vancouver. Her practice focuses on residential projects. From the experience of her own home remodels, she realized the importance of homeowners having a guide. In 2017, she launched Stress-Free Remodeling, wrote the number one best-selling book, The Homeowner's Guide to Stress-Free Remodeling, and created the innovative online program, The Ultimate Stress-Free Remodeling Blueprint. She also hosts the Stress-Free Remodeling

Podcast. You can learn more about her here: stressfreeremodeling.com.

Get Emma's free gift ...

The Remodel Essentials Checklist here:

TeachYourExpertiseBook.com/gifts

Chapter 14
Pivotal Shifts for Making an Impact, Increasing Financial Wealth, and Living a Life of Freedom
by Monica M. Bijoux

I grew up with firsthand experience of how trauma can impact a person for life; how it can shift someone's mindset and cause her to get in her own way as she pursues her goals.

Because my mother never healed from the trauma she experienced in her own life, I was destined to a life of abuse. I also watched how she never completed anything she started, often blaming others for the fact that she didn't achieve her goals. I could see, though, that the real reason she didn't accomplish her dreams was lack of ambition. She was an extremely talented, smart, and creative woman. However, her mindset would get in the way, and she often gave up.

Watching my mother start and stop different projects on numerous occasions, I was determined to live differently. And I knew in order to do that, I had to *think* differently.

Not only did I make a commitment early on to stay out of my own way and pursue my dreams with passion, but I also knew I wanted to help others follow their dreams, too.

It all starts with mindset. Although I hold a variety of titles—licensed clinical social worker, certified master level coach, author, speaker, podcast host, and certified hypnotherapist—helping people with mindset and emotional growth has played a major role in my life for as long as I can remember.

My desire to help others often led to me volunteering and helping my friends in any way I could, including helping them grow their businesses. My volunteering experience later served me well.

In 2006, I was pursuing a master's degree in Human Resources Administration. My professor assigned a presentation on change, and my role was to be a "Change Agent": someone who guided a business owner to make changes necessary for business growth and development.

Fortunately, I had just volunteered to help one of my friends, who was the owner of a computer repair store, to make changes that would result in growth—not only in his business, but also in his personal life.

While talking with the business owner and observing how he ran his store, I noticed several process improvements that had the potential to make the business more lucrative, productive, and professional. I also saw that he struggled to connect with his clients, stay organized, and manage his time and habits. Most of these improvements would require a slight shift in his mindset; he considered the way he ran his business, along with the results he created, as "normal," based on his experiences and a lack of examples of people doing things differently.

I made several suggestions, and when the store owner followed them, he began to create better relationships with his clients and hire professional and productive personnel.

In less than six months, the computer repair business went from receiving a few hundred dollars a week to earning mid-six figures.

As I began to prepare my paper and presentation the night before the school assignment was due, I prayed about how to describe the changes I'd helped the business owner make. I received spiritual downloads of words, which I wrote down on a piece of paper before going to sleep. I woke up a few hours later—just six hours before it was due—to write the paper.

When I awoke and wrote all the words out in my slides in the order the words were given to me, I realized the first letters of all the words spelled DECIDE TO MOVE. I could not believe it, but through prayer, I had developed what I now refer to as the 12 Steps for Change. It also became my transformational model.

Later, when I decided to start my coaching and consulting business, I named my company after my model, and that is how DECIDE TO MOVE LLC (DTM) was born. DTM's mission is to help clients discover their God-given purpose and give them the strategies, knowledge, and confidence to see that purpose through—with excellence. I empower people to work in their purpose, find their truth, and ultimately, create a rewarding, fulfilling life.

Business owners and entrepreneurs hire me to help them get back into the game of their life and business. My clients know they don't have to start at the bottom, because they have already experienced some form of success. They are ready to make a pivotal shift for a more meaningful impact, increase their financial wealth, and have a life of freedom—all while avoiding trial and error. Some of the methods I use to empower my clients to do these things include online programs, masterminds, virtual events, books, and customized plans based on their personality, strengths, and desired destination. All of these include pieces of my transformational model.

I've also applied the DECIDE TO MOVE model to my own personal life in order to create a transformation … and doing so proved to me that it works in *any* area of life. I've taught it to my clients and used it again and again myself, as well.

To continue to grow myself and provide additional value to my clients, I hired a business coach, Alina Vincent, after attending one of her live events. I believe every coach needs a coach to continue to grow personally and professionally.

In September 2018, I attended Alina's High Profit Programs live event, and I learned how to create my first online program. She recommends creating programs to reach more people, make a bigger impact, and grow your business exponentially (and, since you're reading this book, I'm sure you're excited about that potential, right?).

For me, because I'd already done so much of the work around mindset and goal achievement, creating my first program was as simple as following a process outlined by my coach.

My first program centered around overcoming childhood trauma (since that was my specialty in therapy). I considered it a learning experience during which I'd master the process of creating a program based on my experience and expertise. I may make changes to the course and run it again under my therapy practice; however, I'll never offer it through DTM, because DTM is strictly focused on business coaching.

That being said, I learned some valuable lessons on creating online programs.

First, creating an online program gave me the confidence that I could create a course anytime I wanted, and that it could be done live (where I provided coaching with the program) or evergreen (where the client can complete the program at his or her own pace and go through the course without any coaching).

Second, the online program gave me the ability to help my clients in a powerful way while also being able to safeguard my time. Whereas working one-on-one with clients requires me to be present in order to make money, an online program empowers me to help a greater number of people (and generate more income) without the time constraints of being in person, one-on-one.

Third, creating an online program or course required me to create a systemized process. Not only did that give me clarity about how I can help people achieve transformation while avoiding trial and error, but it also gives me the ongoing opportunity to constantly improve upon my process.

Finally, once I had that initial program, I could use it as the foundation for so many other business elements, if I wanted to (or, I could *not* add elements, and enjoy making money and a difference 24/7). I could add coaching, group programs, live events, and more. The options are endless!

Clients loved it, too. They talked about how they were able to digest the information at their own pace, which enhanced their transformations. Rather than struggling to keep up or waiting around for the next lesson, each participant could process what I shared at a comfortable pace that complemented whatever was going on in his or her life. Clients shared that they experienced dramatic changes, quickly—more quickly than they would have if they were in therapy or doing one-on-one coaching.

Hearing from people who went through my first online program, **Overcoming Childhood Trauma and Setting Boundaries**, was a powerful reminder that I could make a big difference even if I wasn't meeting with people one-on-one.

For example, one of my clients who went through that program said she was a little hesitant when she considered enrolling, because she'd already been in and out of therapy for a few years, and felt she might need it continuously.

She thought the coaching she received in my program might be too similar to therapy to make a difference for her.

"Not only did I get some of the best advice," she said after completing the program, *"but I also had time to self-reflect and relate to other women in the program. Monica is truly invested, which shows in how she builds upon certain topics and makes sure everyone leaves the program with value added to their life.*

"This last year, I had been struggling with the biggest heartbreak of my life. Her coaching was able to show me how my childhood trauma affected my relationships, even those not romantic in nature. I am still working on reframing my self-doubts and learning to set appropriate boundaries with the appropriate people, but that's the great thing about coaching: I now have the tools to continue improving long after the program is over. Since the program has ended, I have been able to start dating in a way that lets me only give the energy I choose to give and to be firm in my boundaries, while also not building my wall too impenetrable."

The reason this program—and my business-building programs, which are my focus now—work so well is because *they focus on creating healthy, empowering mindsets*, which then opens my clients up to absorb the strategies and implementation necessary to reach their desired destination.

That being said, I'd like to share some powerful perspective on mindset from my Millionaire Mindset Secrets resource, to empower you to get started in creating a healthy mindset rich for achieving any goal in any area of your life.

Have you ever wondered what sets apart the people who seem to be able to achieve anything they want to? The people who earn a great living, find a great partner, have good, lasting friendships, and seem so happy?

Have you thought about what sets apart successful people from those who struggle?

Rich people from poor?

It's mindset. Mindset is *the* number one factor in determining what kind of life you'll have—whether you'll reach your goals, get what you want, and feel fulfilled.

Rich, happy, successful people think differently.

What can you do to cultivate a mindset that will empower you to create everything you want?

Step 1. Think positively. That which you focus on, grows. Concentrate on what you want to be, have, or do. *The more you* *focus on it, the more your subconscious mind will help you achieve it.*

Step 2. Create your own path for success. Let go of the mindset and belief that you have to reach success in exactly the same way someone else did. Following others may create initial success, but in order to achieve success that feels fulfilling to you, **you must follow your own voice and create your own path**.

Step 3. Love yourself; believe you're worthy of the things you want. If you don't feel like you deserve the best, you'll never be able to work toward it or achieve it; your subconscious mind will continue to sabotage you (if you've ever begun creating results or making strides toward a goal, only to backslide and lose momentum and progress, you know what I'm talking about!). *Believe it— because you do!*

Step 4. Do what you love doing. If you're stuck in a job you don't enjoy, you won't work hard. No matter how long you spend in this job (daily, weekly, yearly, and so on), you won't be truly successful. *Figure out what it is that lights you up, and then, start creating the path to do it.*

Step 5. Let go of jealousy. Jealousy is a negative emotion and will only attract more negativity (and lack). If you're experiencing jealousy, you'll be diverted from the path of achieving the kind of abundance you desire. Focusing on what another person is doing or what they have will keep you from being able to focus on your own goals, dreams, and ambitions. *Concentrate on the habits they are displaying, instead, and asking how instead of why.*

Step 6. Take responsibility for what happens in your life; don't blame others! As you'd take credit for your successes, you also must *take responsibility for your failures and identify what you can do differently going forward.* Adopting this mindset will help you to always take the lesson from a failure (or a less-than-perfect success), so you continually focus on growth.

These six steps will help you begin cultivating a healthy mindset, which, as I mentioned earlier, will help you achieve any goal you set … including creating an online program!

As you may have guessed, cultivating the right mindset is my first piece of advice when it comes to creating an online program, too. Once you have the right mindset, anything is possible!

And again, while I know many people struggle with self-doubt and/ or overwhelm when they consider creating a program, I didn't (I simply followed the steps my business coach outlined), and I'm confident I was able to do so seamlessly because I already had a solid, positive mindset in place.

In addition to cultivating your mindset, you'll want to also dig deep and identify your own expertise, passion or purpose—the life-changing lesson or system you have to share—as you begin creating your own online program. When you know your own strengths and passions, you're more easily able to move on to the next step, which is to get crystal clear on who you want to serve.

Defining your ideal client goes beyond demographics like age, career, and number of children. It's about identifying your clients' biggest problem (related to your expertise) and putting into words (words they'd use and identify with) how you can help them solve it.

Connect your expertise/passion with what your ideal clients want, and you will have a winning combination!

Following these steps myself, I recently created a program more closely aligned with my current passion—helping business owners and entrepreneurs build authority, grow their audience, and attract more clients with podcasting. It's called How to Launch a Profiting Podcast in 30 Days. I'm so excited about it, because I believe podcasting is a fantastic avenue for sharing powerful messages, reaching your ideal clients, and increasing financial wealth.

Creating a program is easier than you may think. And I hope, now that you've heard my story, that you feel inspired … inspired to shift your mindset, become empowered, and begin changing the world in a bigger way than ever before.

* * *

Monica M. Bijoux is a best-selling author, podcast host, certified master coach, trainer, speaker, and the founder and CEO of DECIDE TO MOVE LLC. Monica's impressive lineup of degrees and special trainings and certifications has allowed her to integrate her passion for helping entrepreneurs gain confidence and clarity and establish personal and professional boundaries. You can learn more about her here: decidetomove.com.

Get Monica's free gift …

Millionaire Mindset Secrets to discover eight more powerful exercises for transforming your mindset, so you can achieve anything and everything you want to here:

TeachYourExpertiseBook.com/gifts

Chapter 15
Hay, Relax!
by Laurel Watson

"Once we stop pressuring our horses to do what we want and instead ask them why they can't do what we ask, this world will be a better place for both humans and horses." ~ Laurel Watson

The request was simple enough: introduce yourself and what you do to the other people at your table.

"I am Laurel Watson. I am an equine bodyworker and dressage trainer."

"What does that mean?" my table mate asked.

Hmmmm. What does that mean? I assumed it was self-explanatory.

There I was, at Alina Vincent's High Profit Programs live event in a room full of "civilians," and I was the only "horse person" not only at my table, but in the room.

I went to the event because I had been struggling to get my side gig business online for at least two years. I "knew" what to do, but had no idea of how to implement, why I kept getting stuck, or how to move forward and become financially successful.

Despite my background in electrical engineering, having managed million-dollar information system projects for 10 years and writing code for 15 before that, I struggled with marketing technology. I understood what a funnel was. I knew the formula for the classic webinar, sure. I could retrofit my story to the format, but strategically, I had no idea how to make sales. I didn't understand how to implement the entire sales process tailored to my business, so horse owners everywhere would want to buy my online program, Dressage Positively.

I hoped the event would show me how to jumpstart sales of Dressage Positively—a program for riders from any discipline who are new to dressage and want to use a positive approach in their training methods versus the old-school approach of force, pressure, and punishment. I wanted to offer a way for horse lovers everywhere to learn how to create a meaningful connection with their horse.

I figured, *piece of cake.*

I'd go to the three-day event in Reno, pitch myself, pitch my program, and ultimately teach participants how to develop their horses positively in several sequential programs that sold like hotcakes. After all, I'd already done a couple of 5-Day Challenges and was growing my group. Now, I just had to offer the program. Easy peasy, right? That's what all the webinars boasted.

Boy, I could not have been more wrong!

Back to the question that stopped me in my tracks at the event:

"What does that mean?"

The more I learned, the more I learned what I didn't know. It would be a little over a year in Alina's coaching program before I started to really see the entire big picture, and how I could create successful online programs that would work in the horse world.

Completely on the spot, I answered, "You know how when you get a dent in your car and they put it up on the rack to repair the damage? Well, equine bodywork is like that, but instead of removing dents in metal, I remove all of that tension within the muscles and fascia of the horses. And without putting the horse up on a rack. Oh, and I also teach people how to teach their horse to dance without having to use force or whips. I show them a way in which the horse loves to learn, voluntarily offering the movement sought."

Yes! *Not bad*, I thought.

Then came the dreaded follow-up question:

"Horses need bodywork?"

At that moment, our focus was called back to the stage.

Phew, dodged a bullet there, I thought.

Still, I couldn't help but think, *of course horses need bodywork! Why wouldn't an equine athlete need the same support that a human athlete needs in order to succeed? And why don't people intuitively know this?*

As it turned out, this was a huge A-HA moment for me. I realized that I may have to teach people the basics *before* I can pitch my offer to them. It's not enough to just create a program; you have to actually let people know why they need it!

Program #1: Dressage Positively: Intro Dressage Bootcamp

Fast forward a few months.

"Just offer a program and get people to sign up for it before you create it," Alina said. "You'll get paid for creating content."

So easy, it's freakin' hard as hell, I thought!!!

Oh, no, not to create the content. I was all over that. I'd been creating content for over two years by then. I had videos. I had workbooks, diagrams, and infographics. You name it, I have created at least five.

The hard part was putting myself out there and asking people if they were actually interested.

So, I muscled through, and posted some things on my personal Facebook page. And I got a few people to sign up for the first version of my program, Dressage Positively: Intro Dressage Bootcamp.

"JUST get 20 people to sign up," Alina had said.

I got three. I was both overjoyed and utterly terrified at the same time!

Later, I realized that most of the people in Alina's coaching program *already had* businesses they had been working on for years. They had existing clients, email lists, and/or a big following. Most were also working on their businesses full time.

Not me. I was a VP at a bank for 15 years and a software developer prior to that.

I was moving on to my second career, because the stress of the finance industry was slowly killing me. I was also trying to build my equine business on top of 10-12-hour work days.

Oh, and I had just moved from NC to FL, and only knew about five people with horses in my neighborhood!

Still, I was giving myself permission to follow my heart. I had grown up with horses … had them all my life. I'd ridden and trained them on my own.

Why not live my passion, right?

I intended on getting my programs going online while I was still working full time at the bank, so I could generate an income and finally get the heck "out of dodge." I was ready to regain my health.

All with just three clients! No pressure, right?

The actual creation of the program was fun, and working with my three clients was fabulous!

That was the easy part.

The hard part actually came after the course was over.

Because ... then what?

How was I going to get my program in front of more people to buy it?

I went into several online dressage groups and asked if anyone would help me with some market research. I wanted to know what they were having issues with. What words were they using to describe their issues? How could I describe my program in a way that would inspire them to buy it?

Geared with the information the members of that group provided, I was ready ... ready to put my program in front of a larger group of horse owners!

I had to figure out who I had access to.

Since I had finished certification in equine bodywork, I knew lots of folks who had horses and access to horses.

I figured, why not start there?

I created a list of all of the people I knew with horses. Even though a large portion of those people were other equine bodyworkers who were certified in the same modality as me, I was able to grow my community to over 600 in the first year.

Lesson #1 in Creating Your Online Program: Start with what and who you know. Take stock of who you know, who you have access to, and what issues they are having that you can help them with.

Equine Business Community on Facebook

By this time, I had been in Alina's program for three months, and I knew I could easily create a Facebook community.

I created a list of everyone I knew who were somehow related to horses and invited them to the Equine Business Community on Facebook. Then, I asked them if they'd like to get on a call and discuss the issues equine bodywork clients were facing, brainstorm some wording, and talk about how to frame the issues the horse owners were having.

The first call filled in less than a week.

Being the project manager I am, I of course provided an agenda for the call and created some worksheets with questions for the other bodyworkers to fill out while we were discussing the issues.

I didn't think the call would last much longer than an hour.

Well, almost three hours into it, as I was starting to lose my voice, the direction of the conversation took a slight detour.

They—the equine bodyworkers—wanted to talk about the issues *they* were having—not the issues horse owners were having.

It was almost midnight my time already, and I had to work the next day, so I wrapped up and asked the question, "What would help you in your business moving forward?"

Several answered having a group forum, like we had just had, on a monthly basis.

And just like that, Dressage Positively was put on hold, and my Equine Business Builder year-long coaching program was born.

Lesson #2 in Creating Your Online Program: "Ask, and you shall receive." Ask your potential clients what they want. Don't be afraid to talk to people who look, sound, and feel a lot like your favorite client. Ask them questions, too.

Equine Business Builder Program

Three 5-Day Challenges later, I was in the wonderful position of having 12 equine business owners enrolled in my year-long Equine Business Builder Program.

Oddly enough, I didn't have an agenda or outline for it when I started, and for some reason, that didn't scare the bejesus out of me. Nor did it scare the first few who signed up.

They just knew that doing it on their own wasn't working.

The calls and 5-Day Challenges I hosted helped them move forward, and I was fostering a positive and supportive energy in the group.

The thing is, after hosting several free workshop-style calls and 5-Day Challenges for equine bodyworkers, I learned how important it is to be willing to go with the flow in order to get to the root of the problem. The same is true in equine bodywork and training a horse.

I decided to embrace the approach of running my programs as research projects. I asked lots of questions, built relationships, and wasn't afraid of failing.

The beautiful thing is, the reason I wasn't worried or scared or stressed that there was no agenda was because I had figured out why I loved working with women in this capacity. I had stumbled upon my "why."

I truly want to help other women entrepreneurs and business owners succeed in their business.

Every time they have a win, I am genuinely happy for them. And I want that for every woman who finds her way to working with me.

Lesson #3 in Creating Your Online Program: Follow your "why." Approach everything in the process of creating, selling, and running your program as a research project, so you can enjoy the process and move through it without getting caught up in the fear of getting "out there."

Equine Business Blueprint Program

My business (The Hay Relax Academy) is where it is today because of the very first online program I created.

The Equine Business Builder Program helped me find my why.

And that's when I realized my mission:

To help 1,000,000 horses and 1,000,000 women.

The way I can do that is by helping horse owners through my equine bodywork practice, Hay Relax, and my Dressage Positively programs. But, in addition to that, I can also help many, many, many more horses by supporting other equine women entrepreneurs succeed in their equine bodywork businesses. AND, I can help 1,000,000 women by guiding them in building their coaching businesses.

As the months in that year-long program went by and the research around helping women become successful in their equine businesses continued, I found a clear and logical process that, when implemented, had a huge impact on their success.

This is how the Equine Business Blueprint Program was revealed.

If you, too, want to build a successful equine business, here are five steps I recommend to get you on your way:

Step #1: Outline your ideal work life.

The three biggest mistakes that many equine business owners make (and they can apply to your business, as well) are:

1. Not knowing how much money they need to make.

2. Not admitting how much money they want to make.

3. Not including time with their family, friends, and their interests (including their own horses) into their schedule.

Identifying and prioritizing the parameters of your ideal work life is key to having a successful business.

Step #2: Get in front of your favorite clients.

When starting out, so many equine bodyworkers and equine service providers get caught up in the trap of giving away their services for free. They also try to convince top-level riders, trainers, and horse owners why they need to use their equine services. Then, they get tongue-tied and become fearful of not being able to sell their services. In reality, the equestrian world is made up of millions of beginning and intermediate riders and horse owners of all disciplines. So why is it that we're told to go after the big guys, when there are so few of them? Go where the masses are! If you are a dressage rider, join your local dressage club. If barrels are more your style, check out your local horseman's associations and jackpot nights. Go where you have natural rapport in the community, and when you've exhausted that source, look to another.

Step #3: Invite your favorite clients to work with you.

If you fail to actually ask the question, you may be part of what I call the "pushing money away" phenomena. Over and over again, horse owners will reach out to you, but if you don't invite them to work with you, you will never have a thriving practice. Learn to recognize the different phrases horse owners will use to indicate interest in your work, and when they utter those magical words, respond with "I'd love to schedule a session with you and your horse. Does next Monday at 3:00 PM work for you?"

Step #4: Design your demos to sell your services (not your modality or method).

As equine bodyworkers and horse lovers, we all know exactly when we decided to make a career in the equine industry. We saw a demo and fell in love with the process. Offering free demos is such a great tool to find prospective clients; however, what the majority of struggling bodyworkers end up doing during the demo is trying to sell the *modality or process* instead of their services. The Equine Business Blueprint Program has an entire course dedicated to helping you design your equine demo to sell your services.

Step #5: Follow up with potential clients to fill your schedule.

One of the most often-asked questions I get from clients is, "How do I keep clients coming back?" It's also by far the easiest question to answer. At the end of each bodywork session or lesson, train your brain to ask this simple question: "When would you like to schedule your next appointment?" And put that date in your calendar. If, by chance, the horse owner says she isn't ready to schedule the next appointment, then ask, "When would you like me to follow up?" and write that date in your calendar. And obviously, follow up with them again on that date.

Create a Successful Business of Your Own

I hope you've found these tips useful for your equine bodywork practice or business. Of course, there is only so much that fits into a single chapter of one book. I can write a whole book on the lessons I've learned while creating my equine business, but the biggest lesson for me was to lean into my intuition, keep moving forward one small step at a time, and not be afraid to circle back, regroup, and try the same thing over again with course corrections. My sincerest hope for you is that you are inspired and encouraged to keep moving forward with your passion in your business.

Hay Relax! … and create a successful online program to grow your business!

***

Laurel Watson is the creator of the Equine Business Blueprint Program, the Equine Business Builder Program, and the Dressage Positively Programs. Her passion is helping women follow their passions, and her mission is to help 1,000,000 horses by supporting other equine business owners in finding financial freedom in their equine bodywork practices and equine businesses. You can learn more about her here: www.hayrelax.com.

Get Laurel's free gift …

Equine Business Quickstart Guide here:

TeachYourExpertiseBook.com/gifts

Chapter 16
An Ocean of Tears to Living MY Dream
by Jeanne Lyons

I was living the dream!

My job allowed for that dream lifestyle—traveling the world on a first-class expense account, wearing beautiful clothes, speaking in front of international audiences, and eating exotic foods.

I savored mussels in Brussels, escargot in Lyon, paella in Madrid, bratwurst in Munich, and even haggis in Edinburgh. I learned how to pronounce "Edinburgh" like a native, and in fact, greet and thank people in every language.

And that was just one seven-day trip.

Upon my return from my travels, there waiting at the airport for me would always be a limo driver holding a sign with my name.

Sounds incredible, right?

Here's what they don't tell you about this "dream job" (lessons from Spain):

- Jetlag is real, and not fun.

- Traveling with a demanding client can be exhausting and sometimes downright embarrassing.

- The cab drivers in Madrid are not required to know English even if they are driving you around for three-and-a-half hours looking for an open restaurant.

- There ARE no open restaurants at 5:30 pm in Madrid even if you are the head of the biggest blockbuster drug in the world and that's when you're used to eating dinner in New York City.

- The female head of the company is La Presidenta, *not* El Presidente, as one is quick to correct.

- In most instances, the bull is not going to get out alive.

There's more:

- You will be expected to jump when they say, "jump." (Like when you find out at 9:00 am that you need to be on the red eye to Chicago even though your daughter has her first school dance that night.)

- When you head a global project, you are *always* on the clock.

- When they do a reorganization at the top, the s&%t almost always rolls downhill.

- And, should you meet with a catastrophic event (like, for example, returning from a whirlwind trip to your fiancé succumbing to cancer two weeks later), the re-org likely won't care enough to keep from sweeping your department clean, replacing you.

All of this was why I cried an ocean of tears flying across the Atlantic in March of 1999.

Secretly, I was relieved to be unemployed. The exhaustion and grief were overwhelming from the two huge losses I had just endured, as well as the loss of my identity. I was no longer betrothed, and I was no longer a world-wide program manager commanding a group of 80 people around the world.

I lost a sizeable salary, too.

My training in the clinical sciences was, of course, very scientific—steeped in procedure and logical steps that lead to an outcome. I tried to use that logic to decide my next steps in gaining new employment.

The headhunters provided me with quite a few promising opportunities.

So, I went to a couple interviews. I figured since I lived in one of the most expensive housing markets in the country, I would be able to afford a very nice house in a new location. You know, something with two master suites, an open floor plan with more square footage than two people needed, and a pool with a spa.

Driving back from the last interview, I remember feeling torn and confused about which job I'd take if I received both of the offers I was expecting, as per the headhunter. Using all my logical tools to try and figure it out, I suddenly found myself calling out in frustration, *"Universe, I give it up to you."*

This was so not like me!

I never wanted to give up control. I was 49 years old and a scientist. I managed large groups of people for prestigious institutions like Stanford University Hospital and made decisions for them all the time—and good decisions, too. Why, now, was I asking for help from such an enigmatic source?

Strangely, I felt a calm come over me.

The next morning, the call I had been waiting for came. Both the headhunter and I were surprised to learn that the one job had decided not to fill the position and the other decided I was not a fit after all!

Oh. My. Gosh.

Now what?

I was standing there in a kind of shock when the phone rang again.

It was the hypnotherapy school I had applied to, telling me a spot had opened in their previously filled class.

I couldn't believe it.

My fiancé Joe's Aunt Bettina had introduced me to the world of holistic/alternative practices when we lost him. I had applied for the school shortly after.

Was this the Universe giving me my answer? I certainly believe so!

I threw myself into my studies and added a whole array of additional modalities. I received the highest certifications in Neurolinguistic Programming (NLP), hypnotherapy, Time Line Therapy®, Emotional Freedom Technique (EFT), Be Set Free Fast (BSFF), Reiki, and was also certified as an Integrative NLP coach by the Association of Integrative Psychology.

Starting a private therapy practice in 2000 was fairly easy. All I really needed to do was hang a shingle, and *Self Synergy* was born.

Seeing clients one-on-one wasn't the most efficient way to make money, though, so I leveraged my time by teaching classes. The marketing was simple enough, sure—it was just a matter of posting a few flyers in grocery stores and coffee shops.

The challenge was doing it ALL myself.

I found it easiest to go back to work in a hospital laboratory part time for the steady paycheck and healthcare benefits. I continued to see one-on-one clients in my *Self Synergy* practice on the side.

In 2004, I decided to use my business expertise and pivot my practice to a more business-focused theme. I launched *Accelerated Synergies*, operating under the premise that by working together, or synergistically, an outcome can be reached more quickly. I worked with alternative practitioners to help them get their businesses aligned with solid business practices.

Through further self-evolution, and while continuing to work my full-time hospital job, my passion became helping women who, like me, were frustrated and burnt out by their highly stressful jobs. They are in midlife, and still excel at what they do (and have done) for years … probably decades. They are still defined by their career. Many have no idea what else they even want to do, let alone what they could do, if they could even figure out how their skills can transfer to another career.

What they do know is that they can no longer tolerate what they are doing now.

I help them become fulfilled by having their life define their career, not the other way around. I help them find a career with meaning and purpose, and if they choose, a legacy.

And now, instead of living "the" dream, I'm living "my" dream, and I couldn't be happier!

Now, with this shift in my business, marketing practices changed radically. I knew who I wanted to reach, but getting clients was no longer as simple as putting up flyers. The internet and digital marketing were flourishing, and it seemed overwhelming to try to figure it out on my own. I knew I needed to get some help and advice.

And again, the Universe lead me to the "who."

I decided to participate in as many free 5-Day Challenges and webinars as I could to learn as much as possible. I found a lot of good information, and I discovered my biggest marketing holes. Even better, because these types of Challenges often offer a brief, free coaching session as a drawing prize, I was lucky enough to win a 30-minute session.

A quick side note, here, about free resources and sessions: take advantage of them! You'll be amazed at what you might learn. They're so helpful, in fact, that I've worked them into my own business model. Here is a summary of one of these sessions I had with a woman from South Africa:

"Najma phoned for an exploratory consultation. She's been in her position as an Administrative Assistant for 16 years and desires more responsibility and a shift into management. On top of maintaining her job, she was managing the end-of-life care for her terminally ill mother who was her touchstone for making decisions. As she relayed her job and life duties, it was easy to see she had extraordinary organizational skills which easily translated to leadership traits. Once I was able to help her see this, it was a fairly simple reframe to give her the clarity and confidence to move forward in seeking the management position she desired."

You see, being formally trained in scientific disciplines gives me the analytical skills to look objectively at my client's qualifications. My alternative and holistic skills allow me to support my client's mind-shift needs. Getting valuable insights like this is common during an exploratory call!

I also realized I needed more support than what I could get for free. I needed to make an investment in myself as well as my business.

Once I found a coach whose style and expertise I resonated with, Alina Vincent, I confidently invested in her programs. I loved the way they were structured and run, and when the offer to attend her big High Profit Programs live event surfaced, I jumped on it.

The topic of the live event was, of course, online programs. I wasn't totally sold on the idea, although I did know I wanted to—*needed* to—leverage my business. So, I paid attention.

I started playing with title ideas while at the event. I remember standing at the mic to try them out on the audience. Thankfully, I'm not thin-skinned.

When it was time for the audience to vote, everyone gave my titles a "thumbs down." Then, a woman in the audience shouted out, **"Burnout to Bliss."** And thumbs went up! I loved it, and decided right then on that title for my online program.

Attending that event taught me two important lessons. The first is the power of the collective brain and a mastermind. There were about 200 people who helped contribute to the title of my program. The second was the importance of having a program.

I also knew I needed help developing one. I took a leap and invested in Alina's Rising Stars Mastermind.

We were given a month to create and launch a pilot program! It was no walk in the park … but, I had a *great* feeling of accomplishment when it was finished.

The biggest obstacle I had to overcome in its creation was to give up my preconceived ideas of how my coaching practice was structured. I had to trust Alina's expertise, which is ironic, because that's precisely what I ask of my clients.

The beautiful thing is that letting go of the control essentially gave me more power. It allowed me to see more possibilities beyond those of my own construct.

Another obstacle I had to overcome was in relation to my commitment to providing a bespoke experience for my clients. I worried that something "chiseled onto tablets," so to speak, wouldn't give my clients the customized experience they wanted.

As it turns out, that's not the case at all. A program is a method for getting your client to a place of competence *before* you start working together in a long-term coaching arrangement. Plus, you can bonus your coaching package clients with the program and be able to jump right in and get started without a lot of preliminary work! It's really a win-win situation. It saves you time and gives the client even more perceived value.

In the end, the program I created became the foundation of my entire coaching practice! The modules give my clients the basis for digging deep to really determine not only what they want in a career, but *why* they want a new career.

It allows me to reach more people with my work, too... people like Mandi Mann, who said, *"Jeanne is skillfully adept at helping me focus on what is really important to me. She helped me figure out steps I need to take to accomplish my goals."*

And Suzanne Salcido. Unexpectedly laid off from her job and her last child at home getting ready for college, she said this after our work together: *"I think the program is fantastic. Sometimes we get lost in the weeds, and it's really good to look at what's important. Particularly in this time of your life, I didn't really think I would be here, but here I am!"*

And Debra Hubers-Paradis, who said, *"With Jeanne, I am happy to say I have combined all my skills/tools into a holistic business that makes my heart sing and make a difference in people's lives."*

If right now you're thinking, "I wish I could move from j-o-b to a career that makes my heart sing," you're in luck!

Here's a simple exercise to help you determine your desired meaning and purpose in your work:

Drawing three overlapping circles to create a Venn diagram. Label one of the circles "Interests," one "Strengths," and one "Values."

Begin filling in each circle to see which items land in the sweet spot—in the center, where the circles overlap. That's the sweet spot for meaning and purpose!

Another exercise I walk my clients through is to determine their "why"—the most important step in determining a career/job change.

Answer these questions:

1. What is making you unhappy with your job?

    a. Is it the environment?

    b. Is it the people? Your boss?

    c. Is it the schedule?

    d. Is it the corporate culture?

    e. Is it the compensation?

    f. Do you like what you do, but not where you do it?

    g. List any others that come to mind.

2. Taking the above into consideration, what can you do to make your current job more pleasant?

   a. Can you change your workstation?

   b. Can you find something good to highlight in order to compliment a co-worker or your boss?

   c. Can you ask for a schedule adjustment or work remotely a day or two a week?

   d. Is there a task force you might start or contribute to that would enhance the corporate culture?

   e. Can you ask for a raise?

   f. Can you ask for a challenging assignment?

   g. List any others that come to mind.

3. What do you like about your job? What makes you go in to work?

   a. Is it the money?

   b. Is it your schedule?

   c. Is it the commute?

    d. Is it the benefits?

    e. Is it something else?

4. Does your job allow you to keep balance in your life?

5. Do you feel fulfilled in your job?

Answering these questions will help you determine whether you can stay in your job, look for the same type of position in another institution, change your career altogether, or consider a life change.

Here is of course a HUGE caveat: changing to just any j-o-b may change your life in the short run, but not for the long haul. If you are desperately unhappy, you are more than likely to make the same career mistakes that got you into this frying pan to begin with. To avoid jumping into the fire, it's important to really dig deep on these issues and get some outside and objective help.

Consider this: If what you needed to do was already in your head, you would have done it already! Seek an outside source. Someone I greatly admire once told me, "Don't ever hire a coach who doesn't have a coach." I have six of them! And each has a special expertise, like copywriting, mindset, business, marketing, etc. The amount of time, money, and frustration you will save will amaze you.

Finally, if you already have a business or are considering starting one, consider the power of an online program.

I'm actually a little embarrassed to share this with you ...

It took me almost a year to realize how incredibly valuable it was to create my program. I was sitting in another mastermind group when the 'aha' moment hit me.

Now, as I mentioned, I use my program to structure almost my entire coaching model. The material lends itself to structuring not only my coaching packages, but also my VIP days. My packages are still customized, but having this structure makes it easier to communicate with my clients *and* helps lend credibility.

I'd love to leave you with my top three tips for creating a program, based on the lessons I learned when creating mine:

1. Build upon logical steps and begin with simple concepts. Don't overwhelm your students or yourself by including too much information.

2. Save some learning for a more advanced program while giving them enough value. Once you develop your first program, you might find you have enough content for even more.

3. The more programs you develop, the more leverage you will have in your business.

Whether you're just starting out and seek clarity in your business, or you're looking for a way to build your existing business, a program might be your perfect next step.

***

Jeanne Lyons is a best-selling author, international speaker, and coach. `She has walked the path of a mid-life career change and come out on the other side with a career with meaning and purpose. She's devoted to coaching you to do the same. To learn more about Jeanne and her programs, go here:

AcceleratedSynergies.com

Get Jeanne's free gift …

The ABCs of Making a Confident Career Change Checklist for practical tips on developing your strategic career plan here:

TeachYourExpertiseBook.com/gifts

Chapter 17
Tapping into Your Body's Inner Wisdom to Accelerate Your Success
by Antonia Van Becker and Greg Lee

My partner Greg sat in his doctor's office in disbelief, still sick with a serious intestinal problem six months after returning from a business trip abroad. He'd seen three specialists who had done multiple tube-down-the-throat tests measuring every imaginable fluid in his body, and after being put on four different prescriptions, he had lost 40 pounds.

His doctor calmly delivered his diagnosis: there was nothing medically wrong with him.

At that moment, Greg knew it would be up to him to get healthy. He left the office, threw his current prescription in the garbage, and started home.

Starving as usual, he stopped at a new grocery store, Whole Foods, to get some munchies. Grazing the aisles, he came face to face with a healer he knew from years before.

"I've been meaning to call you," he greeted her.

She looked him straight in the eye and said, "I know. Your pancreas is really in trouble."

Greg made an appointment with her, getting in on a cancellation, and in just one session, *all his symptoms were completely healed!*

It was miraculous … and intriguing.

That intrigue sparked the beginning of our healing business, Self Health Institute. Together, we trained and apprenticed with our healing mentor, learning the beautiful energetic healing that became (and has remained) the core of our business.

In 2007, twelve years into our business, we took over teaching our mentor's two-year certification program, which led to many new realizations.

Our mission—to help millions of people heal from life's adverse experiences—was taking shape, and a new vision of our business was beginning to emerge. It was time to address the unfulfilling symptoms of procrastination, self-doubt, fear, and chronic illness on a larger scale.

It was also a time of family transformation and upheaval. Seven years into our four-generation cohabitation experience with our then high school daughters, my aging parents, and my 103-year old grandmother, it happened.

Our lives imploded.

Our oldest daughter got in with the wrong crowd and started using drugs. Things went downhill from there.

To pay for several rehabs and her continued treatment, we fell into a black hole of credit card debt. We started working harder, longer hours—nights, weekends, and even weekend nights!

After what seemed like forever, we crawled out of debt, exhausted. We knew we had to come up with another way of doing business that would let us work with more people at a time, like leading more workshops and teaching more courses. That's when we began investigating the world of online marketing for our business.

It looked intriguing and exciting, but, boy, did we have a lot to learn! We were "going in empty," so to speak. We had no online presence, a very small newsletter mailing list, and no experience in online marketing. What we *did* have were some unique skills we learned in Silicon Valley and from our business backgrounds.

For years, I had managed a large internal technical training department, and Greg had managed a music software sales department. So, we jumped, or rather, got *pulled* in. We knew online was where we needed to go, and quickly realized we didn't know what we didn't know.

I joined Alina Vincent's "Fast, Easy and Profitable Online Challenges" program, and as a result, we got our first client for our online program that didn't exist yet!

YIKES!!!

That meant we absolutely HAD to develop a program.

But despite our vast teaching experience, neither of us had ever done so before. And now, we'd be doing it as a team.

After taking several courses on how to develop online courses, we came up with a name, logo, course platform, and a million other things, all while trying to stay sane *and* friends.

Having been married for over 30 years at that point (yes, married as children!), it was still very challenging. Working so closely brought up issues we didn't even know we had! And the bigger our goals became, the more our hidden fears, negative thinking, and outdated beliefs came out, many times directed at each other.

For example, I remember seeing my picture on a banner for the first time at a public speaking gig. It freaked me out! I had a fear of being seen. I knew I was kind of shy and an introvert, but hadn't recognized it as full-on fear and self-doubt! And Greg began to see how his perfectionist attitude made him feel like he wasn't prepared, especially when it came to making sales calls.

These unhealed challenges made it hard for us to move forward as quickly as we wanted to.

Still, we determined failure was not an option. We started using our healing methods on ourselves and cleared out stuck emotions and limiting beliefs to overcome our internal challenges.

Most interestingly, as we developed our online programs, we also learned even more about our own skills and areas needing development. For instance, because of our backgrounds, Greg was more comfortable in sales and marketing. He learned how to make invitations to our perfect clients, so it was a natural fit. He also found a love for working with joint venture partners and jumped right in to expand our reach! Because of my background in training, I focused on course development and learned how to develop highly effective online courses (with Alina's help, of course) that were fun AND transformative.

We learned to play to our strengths and unique skills, divide and conquer the tasks, and be kind to ourselves and each other. Those are the rules we still play by today as partners in life, love, business, and music!

Our first online program, **The Ultimate Self-Healing System**, was born in 2018. Participants learned to engage their bodies' inner healing systems to heal core issues and get healthier, happier, and more focused, giving them more time, clarity, and abundance.

And because our course was online, we could reach so many more people than before. We have clients around the world, and can work with them regardless of what's happening in the world. We teach, coach, and do healing sessions online. And, most beautifully, our busy clients do our courses from the comfort of their own homes when their schedule allows!

We believe that by teaching, you learn. And that maxim is multiplied when you teach online! Not only do you continue to learn about what you're teaching, but you learn about your own skills and competencies, so you can help others do the same. We're *still* discovering our unique superpowers to increase our impact AND our reach!

By working with more people online, we get to see the wonderful transformations our clients go through. Our client, Linda, a heart-centered financial prosperity coach, said this:

"Growing up, I learned what to say and what not to say to stay out of trouble and keep the peace. As a result, speaking up for myself, standing up for myself, and feeling seen and heard have long been my growing edge. After working with Antonia and Greg, and using The Ultimate Self-Healing System, I experienced an immediate and significant shift. I've had my own business and, for many years, alternated between marketing and hiding—not an effective combo! Since working with Antonia and Greg, I've felt centered, clear, and confident. Self-doubt and second-guessing myself have been replaced by simply sharing the best truth that I know. As a result, I'm feeling seen and heard in situations where my ideas and opinions had previously been dismissed without consideration. Antonia and Greg are truly gifted healers with an incredible understanding of the inter-relationship of physiology, energy, and emotions. They are kind, caring people with deep integrity."

She later shared that she had also gotten a new higher-level position with a big pay raise as a result of her changed presence!

So many people suffer from self-doubt, procrastination, perfectionism, and overwhelm, just like Linda had. If you can relate, here are a few of our favorite tips for staying focused on our unique skills and moving quickly toward our goals and dreams while staying energized, confident, and healthy.

Tip 1: Practice "True North" Goal Setting.

I've always wondered why some people are super successful and others are not. And of course, there are a variety of reasons: certain people may be sales and marketing wizards, while others may offer their program or product with perfect timing for the market, and some have a personality that people just seem to flock to.

But what we have seen, after years of working with clients, is that successful people set goals. Now, we're not talking about one-off, "I want to have a million-dollar business" type goal. We're talking about creating a vision and setting goals to realize that vision. It's also about setting the *right* goals on a regular basis, making them measurable and achievable, writing them down, and tracking them!

Goal setting and tracking has an amazing way of bringing attention to what we desire as well as an understanding of what is standing in the way of getting what we most desire.

And as we take steps, specific actions to achieve specific goals, we realize our unique skills and how achieving those goals serves us in a unique way.

And here's where the goal-setting magic sauce comes in:

When you make and pursue goals that are perfect for you, you find the right strategies, partnerships, and niche for your business or program, and work seems more like play. What we want to minimize are the times we work really hard to complete an entire cycle in business only to find that doing it made us miserable, and wasn't what we actually wanted at all.

In our online program, **The Success Accelerator Code**, we use powerful tools and simple processes to tap into your body's inner wisdom to ensure the goals you are working toward are your "True North" Goals. Then, we clear whatever is standing in your way of achieving those goals, whether it's procrastination or fear, self-doubt or limiting beliefs, or emotional trauma, so you can use your unique skills to bring your powerful and transformative offering to the world.

Tip 2: Cultivate Emotional Awareness.

Are you aware of your thoughts, feelings, and beliefs? Do you observe what you're thinking and feeling? If so, you are cultivating emotional awareness.

When we have emotional awareness, we see evidence of how we're affected by not only the experiences that are happening in the moment, but even more so by what happened to us in the past.

The Center for Disease Control's Adverse Childhood Experiences study proved that adverse experiences in childhood negatively impact health and happiness. That study, conducted with 17,500 people, concluded that the major factor in the development of disease and disfunction (heart disease, diabetes, high blood pressure, alcoholism, eating disorders, suicide) for an individual is the occurrence and frequency of adverse experiences (violence or abuse, divorce, drug addiction, neglect, death of a parent or sibling, mental illness).

Healing the effects of these adverse experiences so our clients can excel in their entrepreneurial journey is what our work is all about.

In our 25 years working with clients, we've seen that these experiences don't just happen in childhood. Our clients continued to have new "adverse experiences" as adults that also affected their business ventures, relationships, and ultimately, their overall happiness and wellbeing.

So, what can we do to minimize the effect of these adverse experiences? Being emotionally aware of how and why we're reacting to the world around us is at the heart of being able to change how we address challenges in our work, life, relationships, and in our health.

Underneath our reactions is the complex layering of how we feel, what we think, and what we believe. When we can step back and look at our thoughts in a difficult moment, it's a very enlightening overview of our state of mind.

Do you go to fear or anger, or perhaps grief when confronted with certain situations? Do you think negatively about yourself or your fellow business associates? Are you always stressed out? Perhaps you don't think you can charge as much as you'd like for your services, even though you're giving a lot of value, because maybe deep down you doubt you're worth it.

Don't despair! These things happen to all of us!

I grew up in a family with alcoholism, drug abuse, and suicide. I didn't realize until much later that being constantly stressed out, always thinking of the worst-case scenario, and developing digestive issues and chronic bronchitis all resulted from living in a disruptive, dysfunctional family.

It was only when I started looking at what I was thinking and feeling, as well as how my beliefs affected how I felt about myself and the world, that I was able to begin healing and changing the way I reacted to the situations I found myself in.

Greg and I often ask ourselves questions like, "*How do I feel about that? What emotion(s) am I feeling? How is that feeling in my body? Is this the right thing for me?*" We also look at how those feelings lead to behaviors that may not be in our best interests.

Cultivating emotional awareness is an integral part of our online courses, ongoing coaching programs, and live events, because we can't change what we aren't aware of. Using emotional awareness as a tool to see how our feelings, thoughts, and beliefs affect our actions gives us an enormous head start on how we can positively affect our outcomes in business, life, and health.

Tip 3: Understand the Impact of Outdated Beliefs.

Wow! You've come so far!

Perhaps you're now setting goals that, if completed, will result in progress that will move your business forward. And you're becoming more emotionally aware, so you can optimize your actions and reactions for a successful entrepreneurial journey!

But what if, in the midst of getting important stuff done, one action, say making those high-end offers, seems impossible to do? No matter how many times you write it down as an important goal, things seem to always get in the way: the kids, the dog, the technology screw-ups, or just checking your email. Pretty soon, it falls off the list, because it just isn't happening.

What we've come to understand, as I imagine you may have too, is that we all have thousands of beliefs that form the basis of who we are and what we do. Our beliefs give us our values and morals; they are the angel and devil on our shoulders, and they are the foundation from which we make all our decisions.

And they can evolve as we grow and change … **OR NOT!**

Outdated and limiting beliefs limit our success in business, life, love, and health. Decoding them can change a difficult task from "Never done" to "Did it today!" Encoding positive beliefs is at the core of a successful business and a happy, healthy life.

So, what are your limiting beliefs? Are they in your way? Understanding that they may be running the show is the first step. Decoding and changing those beliefs is the next step toward abundance and wealth!

Our lives and entrepreneurial journey have changed since we created our online course, Success Accelerator Code, which gives people a step-by-step process to discover and *heal* core issues to eliminate procrastination, self-doubt, fear, and outdated beliefs, so they can have more time, success, abundance, AND a renewed sense of self-worth.

We've learned so much about ourselves, our clients, and how quickly massive transformation can happen!

Whether you're a coach, healer, writer, speaker, entrepreneur, or solopreneur, there's a way to bring what you offer into the online world.

And if you're thinking about creating an online program to grow your business—something we believe is a vital aspect of every business in the modern world—use some of the tips above to experience less stress and more health and happiness.

Remember: take a breath ... be right here, right now ... and feel into yourself. Feel the uniqueness that makes you most decidedly you! Feel your genius, your superpower, your North Star, and make *that* your program. It'll be perfect.

We've gained so much exposure worldwide by going online, by embracing the challenges that this platform offers, and by jumping in with both feet into this brave, new world!

And we trust that you can, too.

* * *

 *Antonia Van Becker and Greg Lee are the founders of Self Health Institute, Inc. For 25 years, they've been using their signature CoreTalk therapy to guide conscious entrepreneurs and business owners toward successful completion of their goals and dreams by asking simple questions and getting life-changing answers. They love helping clients get past overwhelm, procrastination, self-doubt, and chronic health issues, so they can have the business and impact they so deeply desire. Together since 1979, their 40-year relationship imbues their healing practice with love, body/mind consciousness, and emotional/energetic balance and awareness.*

Antonia and Greg live their dream in the wilds of West Marin, California, healing others, growing food, and writing songs to inspire others to envision and realize their dreams. You can learn more about them here: www.selfhealthinstitute.com.

Get Antonia and Greg's free gift …

3 Common Blindspots That Sabotage Your Success so you can quickly spot and shift common roadblocks that often derail your ability to get things done quickly and easily here:

TeachYourExpertiseBook.com/gifts

Chapter 18
Finding Your Power Through Horsepower
by Alisa Clickenger

There are times when harnessing your personal power comes easier than others.

In 1995, in the middle of a painful divorce, I didn't feel I had any power at all. Interesting, then, that my subscoscious conjured up a dream in which I was running away from imminent danger, and riding a motorcycle saved my life.

It was such a magical feeling ... that sense of salvation, of taking back my power and being in control of my own destiny.

At the time, I didn't know that I was lacking personal power, but having a taste of the raw horsepower in my dream state ignited something inside of me. I awoke from the dream knowing in my bones that I *must* learn to ride a motorcycle.

I began with a motorcycle safety course. Learning to ride was challenging, yet something about the mastery of machine continued to call to me. I knew with every fiber of my being that I just had to keep swinging a leg over that saddle and riding.

I never imagined myself doing extraordinary things, let alone where two wheels could take me.

Twenty years later, I've ridden motorcycles on four different continents, traveled solo on two wheels from New York to Argentina, and journeyed around the globe riding, teaching, and participating in events that earlier in my life would have seemed an impossible dream.

Two decades back, I was a shy, introverted housewife living a quiet, sheltered life.

Now these things are my normal.

I have built my personal power through horsepower.

My passion for motorcycling has led me to break through my self-perceived limitations and has empowered me to live a bold, empowered life *on my own terms*.

It wasn't always smooth riding; at times, I've faced many challenges. I had to earn my place in the motorcycle media and marketing field, which I passionately love. I had to learn, fall, and get up again, experiment, fail, and experiment again until I succeeded.

The biggest hurdle for me, however, wasn't that constant perseverence. It wasn't learning my craft as a self-taught journalist, learning to travel well and organize events, or the actual skill of riding a motorcycle. My biggest hurdle has always been a lack of confidence. Self-doubt has ridden alongside me for years, on and off motorcycle, and I have spent many more years building up my self-worth from the shy housewife I once was.

My lack of confidence wasn't always self-evident, though. Self-doubt is deceiving; we can mistakenly turn it inward, thinking we have a defect of character or lack of talent. Think about it: how often do we give up on something, telling ourselves, "*Well, maybe I just don't have what it takes,*" or "*Maybe this isn't for me*"?

You can probably relate. This "problem that has no name" is so widespread among women, I am amazed how little we (still) talk about it.

Confidence, or lack thereof, can make or break us in so many ways. Low self-esteem, self-doubt, and feeling like we aren't good enough can have crippling consequences.

How often have *you* stopped yourself from speaking up, taking a risk, asking for a raise, holding someone accountable for his or her actions, or simply daring to explore new opportunities just because you didn't believe in yourself?

How often have you seen others do something amazing, achieve something you've always dreamt about, or change their lives while you watched from the sidelines, immobilized by self-doubt?

When you look into the confidence conundrum, it turns out that lack of confidence among women is *the number one obstacle* to everything from enjoying a richer personal life, to a better-paying job, to a flourishing career. What does that look like "in real life"? High-powered female CEO's suffer from crushing self-doubt, supermodels often believe they are ugly, and brilliant female scientists and doctors can sometimes experience debilitating uncertainty around their own talent.

Throughout my own journey, I have witnessed how women perpetually underestimate their abilities, talents, and expertise. Also, numerous studies have shown that women are consistently less self-confident than men. According to a Hewlett Packard internal study, women only apply for high-paying jobs when they are certain they have 100% of the required skills, whereas men apply for the same positions when they have 60% of the required abilities (The Road to Discovery: Women and Motorcycles, https://tinyurl.com/confid23875).

Diagnosing a problem is the first step in finding a solution.

Discovering I wasn't alone—that many women experience some degree of lack of confidence unrelated to their expertise or skill, I set out to find ways to boost my own self-confidence.

The truth is, self-confidence gives us the courage to take action and claim responsibility for our own lives. It empowers us and guides us. It helps us to convert ideas into action and transform insecurity into authenticity.

Confidence is looking at something and instead of thinking, *"It's impossible,"* you begin looking for solutions.

Thus, my quest to bring that confidence—a learned skill—to other women began.

Motorcycling became a natural means for my quest, because when a woman starts riding, she finds and is able to access her personal power. When we get engaged in something, we commit. And when we commit, we grow. So, I threw myself into my work, and the discoveries I made along the way became the cornerstones of my coaching business.

Building a strong and diverse community of female motorcyclists through organized motorcycle tours, nationwide events, weekend rides, and one-on-one coaching has given me some great insights into what women are capable of when they begin to truly believe in themselves. I have witnessed women learning to ride and setting out on solo cross-country journeys, embarking on new career paths, transforming their personal lives, creating businesses, taking careers to the next level, and re-discovering themselves.

This is when I realized that if a motorcycle, some confidence coaching, and a little bit of determination can transform a shy housewife into a world traveler and entrepreneur, it can do the same for countless other women out there, too.

All we needed was connection, community, the magic of the road, and some guidance.

And that's what I decided to provide.

As I began working with female riders and getting involved in the motorcycling community more and more, I realized the reach simply wasn't there. There is only so much you can do with motorcycle tours and events.

Although women were certainly interested and eager to learn how to boost their confidence through motorcycling, one-on-one coaching and speaking at events simply wasn't enough.

Enter online programs.

With my webpage and social media platforms getting an unprecedented amount of hits and engagement, I saw how solution-oriented women were online. At the same time, my book, *Boost Your Confidence Through Motorcycling: A Woman's Guide to Being Your Best Self On and Off the Bike*, instantly became an Amazon. com #1 Bestseller when it came out. I was receiving messages, emails, and comments from women all over North America—even some from women in different countries around the globe.

I realized the need for connection and the thirst for adventure among women was much greater than I had anticipated. It was so exciting to grasp that my message was important to so many women around the world!

And that's when I decided to create my **5 Weeks to a More Confident You** online program. While I love guiding motorcycle tours, speaking at events, and organizing retreats, I knew that an online program would be the only way I could offer unlimited, global, and instant reach. I felt it would be a great way to offer women the right tools to boost their confidence in meaningful, impactful ways.

I was also hoping an online program would allow me to grow my business: having one would give me a bit of a breather from all the time on the road in order to connect with my audience.

Creating My Online Coaching Program from Scratch

I always counsel clients to "set a date and speak your objective out loud." Thus committed, I started creating my program at the same time I was promoting it.

Knowing that building self-esteem is a process, I created my online program as an excellent way to *get started* working with clients.

It offers actionable, impactful tools to build confidence on and off the motorcycle.

It's not just about self-love, meditation, or affirmations (although all of those things can be helpful). My approach to building confidence through adventure is threefold: I believe you need to work on your physical, mental, and emotional skills at the same time to get the best results.

Learning the practical skills, such as motorcycle rider training, is the first step. Learning and improving our physical skills naturally helps us build the mental and emotional ones, so we start by looking at each woman's individual journey.

255

Next, we work with our mental and emotional skills, beginning with fear management. Fear is an extremely powerful emotion, and it's important to learn how to distinguish our gut-felt real fears and mental fears that don't serve us. Motorcycling makes this easy, because it's fun and freeing, and we get immediate feedback.

Once we establish the difference between valid concerns and fears that arise from lack of confidence, we can begin the crucial work. Learning to trust ourselves and our decisions, changing our attitudes toward perceived failures, stopping the shrugging off of victories as accidents, and positive self-talk are some of the tools I share.

The juiciest step in the program is transferring motorcycling skills to everyday life skills.

Essentially, I've designed my entire program to help participants experience freedom from self-perceived limitations and begin building bold lives they love!

If that sounds like something you'd love to experience, here's a quick and simple technique you can use any time you struggle with self-doubt, anxiety, or feeling like a fraud to quickly course correct.

Visualization Exercise:

As motorcyclists, we gear up when we ride. We don our safety apparel—jacket, pants, boots, gloves, and helmet. A uniform of sorts, it can also be likened to a superhero outfit.

When you find yourself stuck in self-doubt, in your mind's eye, visualize yourself in your own super-hero costume.

Put your riding suit on, click the helmet visor down, and get ready to ride!

Imagining ourselves as powerful, fierce, and free—the way we feel when we ride motorcycles—can help us conquer life's daily gremlins as well, whether it's a grumpy boss, an impatient child, or a partner who refuses to understand your point of view.

Both of those people can reside within us simultaneously: the woman busy at work who may not feel her full value, and the woman who suits up, swings a leg over the saddle of a motorcycle, and revs the engine of a powerful machine beforeriding off into the horizon.

You've got this!

Digging Deep

The process of creating my first online coaching program was challenging, and at times, I definitely had to dig deep.

The biggest challenge I faced was trying to do it all by myself. As a solopreneur, I'm used to that, and I do it well. Admittedly, I'm my own worst critic and my own harshest boss, and as I started building my online coaching program, it *was* overwhelming.

However, as it is in life—and motorcycling!—you are always learning. The process of creating my online coaching program was instructive, teaching me to focus on the big picture, to delegate, and to learn to accept help from others. It also provided me with incredible feedback from women interested in private coaching.

If you're reading this right now because you're considering creating your own online program, you may think you can do it all by yourself … perhaps that you even *should* do it all by yourself, because it's your "baby."

The reality, however, is that there is no need to try and become an expert in *everything*.

My advice is to focus on what you do best—your coaching, your content, your message—and enlist others to take care of the details. Hire freelancers, join a mastermind … get all the help you need because in the end, what matters at the end of it all is the result you create for your clients … not whether you designed the newsletter format on your own.

In addition, evaluate your time and your resources. Is it worth spending eight hours researching Instagram algorithms, or is your time better spent talking to your clients and polishing your content while a social media professional takes care of your reach?

Another challenge I faced was not getting lost in the details.

It's so easy to obsess over page designs, fonts, and lighting when you're filming your videos. I'm not saying those things don't matter: to a degree, they absolutely do! However, no beautiful font will ever cover up an uninspired message, and no shoddy webpage design will ever overshadow stellar content.

If you are thinking of creating your own online program, always keep your eyes on the big picture! Building a program requires a lot of moving parts to come together. You'll need to think about the technology, the right platform, the design, the marketing, the look … but the most important thing is this:

Never lose sight of the message you are trying to convey.

If your program genuinely helps people, if your mission is relatable, if your solutions are actionable and impactful, people will appreciate them regardless of the packaging.

Remember to always think of your message and your clients first and overdeliver with your work.

All the rest will fall into place.

And yes, you will undoubtedly make mistakes. And that it is okay. You *will* hire the wrong web developer, push back your launch date, change and tweak the content, polish your skills, sometimes get it wrong, and often wish there was a handbook for what you're doing.

Never let fear of making mistakes stop you. Instead, learn from them and move on—stronger than ever before and all the better for sharing your gifts.

That's the beautiful thing about being an entrepreneur! Being nervous is okay. Struggling with imposter syndrome is okay. Just keep showing up and delivering the utmost value possible to your people.

You will learn as you go along, invent and reinvent things, fail, and veer off course sometimes. The end result, however, is going to be absolutely unique, and that is something to celebrate.

When we learn to ride motorcycles, we taste the freedom, the thrill, and the adventure. And then, little by little, we can choose to transfer that sense of freedom and adventure into our normal everyday lives.

We learn to be bolder and ride further than we thought possible.

We become more resilient, more empowered, and more fearless.

Yes, we can still fail at times. However, instead of breaking, we learn to bounce. We ride with our backs straighter and our helmets facing further on down the road.

We begin to live bold, empowered lives we love!

* * *

Twenty years ago, Alisa Clickenger had a dream in which she was running for her life. In the middle of a painful divorce in waking life, she found salvation in her dream state in the form of a motorcycle and sped away from imminent danger. Never having ridden a motorcycle before, Alisa awoke with the sensation of mastery over machine and wind in her hair, knowing she had to break out of her "safe" life and follow her dreams. In 2006, she quit her job as Director of Operations for an IT company and fully embraced her life's mission of inspiring women to be more confident while empowering them to pursue lives they love. Alisa is the author of the bestselling book, Boost Your Confidence Through Motorcycling: A Woman's Guide to Being Your Best Self On and Off the Bike, and offers private coaching to women on and off the bike. You can learn more about her, purchase her book, and/or join her VIP Learn to Ride program here: www.AlisaClickenger.com.

Get Alisa's free gift …

5 Ways to Start Riding Motorcycles and Boost Your Confidence to find your personal power through horsepower here:

TeachYourExpertiseBook.com/gifts

Chapter 19
Staying the Course in Times of Fear and Uncertainty
by Susan Rolfe

As a professional chef of over 30 years, I know what it is to work in the fast lane.

I've taught cooking classes in Italy and baked apple pies in an Indian Ashram. I've worked in restaurants and served as the private chef for the CEO of Starbucks. As a freelance personal chef, I customized meals for over 60 private clients, cooking in their own homes. I catered lavish events, handling not only the food, but the linens, tables, and dance floor, too.

I figured out how to adapt and create in unfamiliar circumstances. I discovered a "flow" that could make work easy and satisfying … even blissful! I also found out the hard way that, when I tried to force things, I burned out. One would think that would have been its own lesson, but with a life-long habit of working through exhaustion, it can be hard to know when to quit.

Then, I was hit with the ultimate challenge:

I could no longer cook for a living. In fact, I could barely walk.

Physical injuries literally put a stop to my cooking career, and I quickly realized what a luxury it had been to have a creative and satisfying skill that I could trade on, just about any time or anywhere in the world.

It was tough to let go of the "chef identity" I had claimed for myself, and all the self-confidence that came with it. I had no idea what to do or how to support myself. The idea of getting a j-o-b after so many years of being on my own was so distressing, I could barely stand to think about it. But it was this very struggle that forced me to let go of the compulsive drive for "bigger, faster, more" in favor of finding "deeper, easier, and more satisfying."

I turned to The Feldenkrais Method to help in my physical recovery, not anticipating the effect the work would have on my confidence and creativity.

Not only was I able to get back into African dance, which had fed my soul for years, but my personal relationships improved and my spiritual life deepened. At the age of 58, I began horseback riding lessons, something I had only ever dreamed of before.

I learned how crucial balance and mobility are to our sense of agency and potency in the world. So often, we don't realize how a sense of grounded safety and calmness is core to our ability to express creativity, passion, and purpose.

I enrolled in a Feldenkrais professional training not only to continue my own healing, but so I could learn to help others heal, too. It felt like the key to my inner peace, as well as the most important contribution I could make in the world.

After graduating, though, I was right back to where I had been before: wondering how to work in a sustainable way. Being a great practitioner clearly was not the same as having a thriving business. Without a way to leverage my time and energy, I was not going to be able to make a living doing one-on-one or group healing work, which was my business model.

So, I invested in coaching, but was still spending a lot of time traveling and money on renting workspace. I quickly found myself in danger of burning out again.

I needed a way to work less and have a better return on my time and energy.

Building an online biz seemed the perfect way to go. But I needed help designing it. That's when I signed on with Alina Vincent.

The problem was, Feldenkrais is unlike anything most people have ever done before. It involves working directly with the brain and nervous system in a powerful, yet subtle, way. Traditionally, this guidance happens one-on-one, or in live, group classes. Could it be effective in the virtual space?

I wasn't at all sure it would work as a home-study program. And, at the time, no other practitioner I knew had an online course.

I was afraid that, since Feldenkrais uses movement, my virtual students would associate it with yoga, pilates, physical therapy, or exercise routines. Of course, if they had not gotten good results with those modes before, they likely would not be open to trying it. Even worse, if they were open to it and actually tried it, but did the movements in the way those other modalities are often taught, they would not get good results, and might even hurt themselves. Then who would they blame? ME!

I certainly did not want them to have a negative experience and then chuck the whole opportunity away. My control issues were surfacing full force.

Luckily, I had Alina's advice: start small, tweak until you see what works, and leverage. Ironically, this is also exactly how I guide my students in learning to move with more precision, ease, and control! It seems obvious now, but I guess I needed to hear my words reflected back in a different context. Once I figured out how to apply Feldenkrais to creating my online course, it felt much safer to begin.

In order to create a virtual program that would meet the needs of those I wanted to support, I broke my lessons down into shorter segments, with simpler and subtler movement sequences.

I used super easy, super slow 'micro movements' that build lasting improvements in core strength, balance, and flexibility. The brain and nervous system are naturally hard-wired to learn this way.

By going slow and building a pattern of success upon success, the body is able to initiate change from within. It's this internal recalibration and return to inner and outer equilibrium that helps them get their life back.

For my people, it is crucial to demonstrate at every opportunity how they can achieve more by doing less. I know this is a mindblower, because it is the very lesson I've had to learn, too!

Building my Better Balance Over 50 online program has had so many benefits. Being virtual reduced travel and expenses, while allowing me to reach more people. The need for simplification and a tighter focus actually deepened my work, making it even more powerful and effective than it was before. And the success I've had has given me the confidence to teach larger groups.

When the COVID19 lockdown hit, I was already positioned to take my "in-person" clients and group classes online and help more people than ever: my engaged audience has tripled over the last six months!

It's ever more obvious that I am not 'fixing' people. Rather, I set up the conditions for them to learn their own best way, from the inside out. The process calms the mind and nervous system. The benefits are global and build on themselves. One woman shared that, as her balance and core stability improved, her carpel tunnel pain disappeared.

Perhaps best of all, participants experience a level of empowerment and confidence that is truly gratifying to witness.

What's not to love?

Here are some of the comments I've received from participants:

" ... *my right hip was pain-free when I awoke this morning, for the first time in about a year. No lie.*" - Cathy Buller

"*I wanted to let you know how much I enjoyed your class. I have not been to a yoga class for 14 months due to hip pain. I had my bad hip replaced two months ago and am finally ready to start exercising. Your class was perfect. In addition to the strengthening, the meditative part of the work was very helpful in this stressful time. Thank you so much.*" - Carolyn Sehler

"Wonderful class! And oh my goodness, walking felt so much easier, too!!" - Alison Eckles

"*The past decade was filled with new health issues for me: unexplained weight gain, an ankle injury that wouldn't heal, arthritis, food intolerances ... a huge cyst. I believe that a lifetime of narcissistic abuse really set the stage for these problems; I was constantly in fight-or-flight mode. I give the work you did with me so much credit for the positive direction my life is going in. It has calmed my nervous system and really opened the door for significant mental and physical healing. I'm not so uberdefensive all the time! I can exercise again! Huge deal!!! A mere thank you can never be enough.*" – Program Participant

Building my program wasn't an entirely easy ride.

The first challenge was to identify who it was for, because Feldenkrais helps EVERYONE! I mean, who doesn't want better function and less pain? I narrowed down who I really liked working with, who responded best, and who got the best results from my micro approach.

My people are over-50 women like me who still have a lot of living to do and value to contribute … but they struggle with falling, pain, and mobility problems. They want to stay independent (perhaps they've seen what happens to others when they can no longer get around, and they don't want to go down that road) and look to the future with confidence instead of dread.

Maybe they've tried PT, yoga, and/or pilates, but keep getting injured. They are not interested in "no-pain/no-gain" plans anymore … they've had quite enough pain already!

Maybe they're used to getting massage, acupuncture, or chiropractic care for pain relief, but for whatever reason, they can no longer get out for hands-on therapy anymore.

Or maybe, they are looking for lasting improvement—like one of my students who said:

"Previously, I've only experienced this type of transformation from acupuncture and sometimes massage, but it doesn't last. I am fascinated to continue."

What they all have in common is a desire to live life to the fullest!

Pretty clear, right? Once I got that clarity, everything was easier.

If you are considering building an online course, too, here are my top five tips for doing so:

1. Get clear on your ideal client. Who are they? What do they want? What specific transformation can you provide? Keep in mind that you can always pivot as you go, too. It's just helpful to be clear on who you're serving and what value you're offering at any given time.

It can be so easy to get caught up in our modality and forget to come from the perspective of our clients. Ask yourself, what are THEIR hopes, dreams, and needs? When you think you've got a good idea, test it out on them.

2. Do less in each part. It's so easy to pack too much in! Do your best to avoid overwhelming your participants. Focus on what they need to know to begin making the transformation you seek for them in a foundational course.

3. Utilize a mix of media (audio/video/images) to maintain interest and cater to different preferred learning modalities.

4. Put disclaimers and legal protections in place. Consult with an attorney who knows what needs to be included to ensure you are not held liable for any surprises you didn't see coming.

5. Get technical help as needed to avoid overwhelm. Unless you are an expert in tech, this is worth outsourcing to avoid unnecessary headaches from things that are not in your wheelhouse.

Going through this process has been one of the most powerful and validating experiences I've had in my business.

By creating an online program, you too can remain mobile, independent, adaptable, and resilient … even in times of fear and uncertainty. And it doesn't have to be hard! In fact, it can be deeply relaxing, creative, and fun.

 *Susan Rolfe is a functional movement specialist and certified Mind Body Studies Practitioner in the Feldenkrais Tradition. She has a passion for helping over-50 women live with more ease, confidence, and joy. She loves African dance, riding horses, and reading mythology. You can learn more about her here:* thespiceoflife.biz.

Get Susan's free gift …

Calm and Grounded For Balance and Ease here:

TeachYourExpertiseBook.com/gifts

Chapter 20
What Are You Going to Do with It?
by Dr. Carol Parker Walsh, JD, PhD

It was my father who placed the entrepreneurial bug in my ear. He would talk to me about the power of creating your own wealth, being your own boss, and the freedom that comes with having control over your life. Now, I admit, when he periodically dropped those gems on me, I thought it was crazy talk! After all, I thought, *weren't you the one spurring me on to get an education and great j-o-b?*

So, despite father's musings about "owning your own," I followed "the model." You know the one … the one that so many of us were raised to adhere to: (1) Go to school, (2) Land a job with a good company (the job didn't matter as long the it was a solid company), (3) Rise to prominence in the company (meaning stay there), and (4) Retire from that same company (having committed your entire life to your work).

After receiving my bachelor's degree in organizational communication and my law degree in employment law, with great anticipation, I started what I thought would be a long and rewarding career as an attorney. The *only* problem was (well, it wasn't the only problem, but we don't have time to go into all that!), I did NOT enjoy the practice of law.

Reviewing "the model," I assumed I went wrong at step 2: "Land a job with a good company." (Sound familiar?) So, I left the law firm in search of the "right" place and became legal counsel with a different organization. While it eliminated some unpleasant aspects of my work, the adversarial nature of law still existed, and that didn't sit well with me.

What I realized was that "the model" never addressed job or career happiness, fulfillment, or satisfaction. Rather, it was based in an economic climate that was rapidly fading away, and today, no longer exists.

My life and career continued to take a few twists and turns, including several moves around the country and the completion of two more master's degrees in organizational development and human development and a PhD in human development and social systems.

As I got older, and more educated, achieving societally acceptable career success, recognition, and respect, I realized that I never quite found the right career for me. I'd either "climbed the ladder" just to find nowhere else to climb, or lost interest in what was at the top of that particular ladder. Or, I leapt onto a new ladder that ultimately led me in the wrong direction.

In retrospect, I recall my father asking me the same question after obtaining each degree: *"What are you going to do with it?"* In other words, how are you going to take that knowledge and make it serve you?

And there it was … that entrepreneurial whisper I heard again and again.

"What are you going to do with it?"

On a recent call with the Department of Labor, they shared that over 65% of individuals polled in the US want to change their careers. The sacrificial nature of "the model" has taken its toll on generations who prioritized career success and financial reward above all else, and frankly, it no longer works. "Jobs for life" is a misnomer, and today, the career ladder looks more like a series of scaffolds that allow an individual to hop from one position to the next, taking their newly developed talent and skills with them.

A man born in the Greatest Generation, it seems my father's words were prolific. However, they didn't truly register with me until I was well into my 40's, following a significant life event.

Recently divorced and settling into my role as "single mother," I remained undeterred in my ambitions and pursuits to be successful in my career. One Sunday evening in February, I was working through another weekend in the office when the guilt hit: my kiddos had to come "play at work" again.

We set out for home, driving down a two-lane road in the rain.

The sun was setting, requiring headlights, as I headed up the hill leading to my neighborhood. Suddenly, I noticed bright lights heading directly at us. Initially believing it was merely a reflection off the wet road, reality quickly dawned on me as the lights barreled straight at us. Cognizant of the fact that I was about to have a head-on collision, and that there was nowhere to escape to on that two-lane hill, I heard a voice say, "TURN NOW!"

Now, my initial thought was *turn where?* To the right of me was a ravine that would send us tumbling down the hill, and to the left, oncoming traffic. Confused, terrified, worried about my children, and truly believing my life was about to end, I simply listened to that voice and made the turn into the direction of oncoming traffic.

Making that turn saved my life.

Our car was hit. Half my body was broken and bruised, and my recovery was long and painful, but here's the truth:

If I hadn't listened to that voice and made that turn, I wouldn't be here today.

I survived because I stopped trying to think or rationalize what I *should* do, and I took action! To be honest, it wasn't the first time I heard that voice in life, but it *was* the first time I listened.

Have you ever heard a voice like that? A whisper in your heart, mind, or gut telling you it's time to make a change? Maybe to do something different in your career? That it's time to TURN?

Have you ever contemplated the simple question, "What are you going to do with that?"

If you're anything like me, and you have heard your own voice, you've likely been trying to ignore it. Why? Because making a turn feels confusing and terrifying. *What about "the model," you may ask yourself.*

You might also know, like I did that day on the road, that if you *don't* "make a turn," the certainty of what's in front of you will become your emotional, mental, and spiritual demise.

It took a traumatic event for me to finally understand what my father had been trying to tell me since I started college many decades ago: to take the road less traveled, and do something amazing with the talents, skills, and education I'd acquired through the years. To enjoy the power of creating my own wealth, being my own boss, and having control over my life.

Now, after an almost 30-year career as an attorney, organizational consultant, executive coach, executive, professor, and dean, I've learned that many woman hear that same voice—the one that says they're meant to do more ... to *be* more. But they don't listen. They don't make the turn, because they're afraid, and the options and alternatives seem less than optimal (at best—even crazy, at worse!).

And that's why I became an executive coach and career and brand strategist.

I get to teach women how to listen to that voice! I show them how to gain the courage to make the turn, step into their life's work, and do what they were meant to do in the world.

You see, if you're like me, a successful, high-achieving powerhouse who often finds herself working nights and weekends in an unfulfilling career, hearing that voice or having that feeling in your gut that's been telling you it's time to make a turn because where you're at just isn't working, then you've landed in the right place, and this chapter is for you.

I'm here to tell you that, while you may not know what will happen when you "make the turn," and even though you may experience some bumps and bruises along the way, what you'll get on the other side is your life ... and the freedom to break free from "the model," so you can do work you love and have a fulfilling and meaningful career.

Reinvention Requires Strategy

My path to teaching, training, and coaching 1000's of women on stepping into their life's work didn't emerge immediately after my accident. It took years of false starts, mistakes, and several course corrections to get here. It's also been the most impactful work of my life.

I'm a social scientist (trained in critical hermeneutic phenomenology) and a critical systems thinker (trained in the Socratic method), so I look for meaning in the lived experience and then work to create a realistic system, or steps, to get the end result. So, while working through my own changes and helping so many other women work through theirs, I've been able to develop a pretty solid and proven system.

After taking my clients through this system with one-on-one coaching, I wanted to construct a way to bring *groups* of women through the process in order to reach more and teach more. In addition, I learned rather quickly that women tend to reach their goals faster when surrounded by a community of collaborative and supportive peers. That type of support is even more critical when embarking on a career pivot or transition, because you'll constantly deal with an inner dialogue of fear and skepticism as well as an outer dialogue from others who will undoubtedly question your move to break from "the model" and live your best life.

With that in mind, I knew I wanted to create an online coaching program. The challenge for me, however, was two-fold. First, how would I condense a year-long system of support into a five- or six-week program? Second, how would I get these highly private, super busy, powerful women to see the power of my methodology in achieving results?

That's when I discovered Marisa Murgatroyd's Experience Product Formula and Alina Vincent's High Profit Programs live event.

Both equipped me with the skills to not only create an engaging program using gamification, which has contributed to a 90% completion rate, but also with the ability to construct an online program that helps my students get the clarity, confidence, and courage they need to get to their desired career path. I decided to name it the **Career Compass™**: a proven system that has helped high-achieving professional women gain the clarity and direction to navigate and pivot in their careers, and step into the career they *really* want.

And it *works*.

Take, for example, Julia Daverne—one of my program participants. After 20+ successful years in the pharmaceutical industry, she decided it was time to retire from the industry and embark upon a new career path. Through her work in the Career Compass™, she *"recognized that her next pivotal career moment had arrived."*

"The Career Compass™ coaching program with Carol has been an amazing and enlightening experience. I have participated in a small collective of amazing supportive women working toward more clarity on their 'true calling' for a more 'integrative life.' If your gut has been telling you it's time for a time-out to reassess your future, I recommend this career-transition program. There is nothing like focused self-assessment to re-evaluate the road you're on with the support of an awesome coach! Carol is unique in her approach to helping you gain clarity, and also in helping you to see how you can leverage where you are to move you closer to what you want. It's a foundational approach to dig deeper. You will find yourself looking at your body of work through a different lens while tapping into strengths you may not realize you have or have forgotten about. This career-transition experience has been what I think most of us 'Midlife Rebels' want and need to do at some point in our lives: to pause and strategically reassess. Thank you, Carol, for all the continued support as I move more clearly and purposefully toward the next phase of my career and a truly aligned and integrative life."

Throughout the process of creating an online program, I was able to crystalize the necessary steps my clients must take to achieve their desired results. By fine-tuning my process, creating the right exercises, and discovering the right pace to present the materials for maximum retention and effectiveness, my program has successfully changed the lives of many women, just like Julia.

Finding the Invisible Thread

On the path toward gaining clarity about their future, my students have to take a walk through their past. The exercise is called Your Life's GPS, and it's designed to illuminate the clues in your own life story that you may have overlooked as key indicators for your future career direction.

If you're in the midst of trying to find clarity on the work you're meant to do in the world, try it out.

Exercise: Your Life's GPS

In this exercise, you're going to look for areas of resonance—to connect the invisible threads of meaning and purpose in your life.

Look back over your life in chunks of 10 years (i.e., 0-10, 10-20, 20-30 etc.), and for each period of your life, write down memories and powerful experiences from your earliest memory until now that made you feel alive, successful, proud, amazing, and filled with joy, love, and happiness. Once you're completely finished, not before, look back over all of that information and find the invisible threads and themes that have emerged, even if it takes a few days. Use a highlighter to circle those threads, to discover key themes and what they say about who you are, where your talent lies, and what types of things bring you joy. You'll be surprised by what you've overlooked for years, but was right there under your nose the entire time!

You may discover an interest in a particular field, industry, or craft that's been with you throughout your life, or a tendency to go for a certain type of job or position (where you are the leader or visionary). What will emerge can reveal your preferences, behaviors, motivators, interests, environments, causes, roles, dreams, past promises, and/or even an entrepreneurial spirit that's been hiding behind fear and the safety of "the model."

Building Your Own Program

It took some time for me to wrap my head around how I could construct a program that would contain all my life's work. However, I constantly remembered my father's question: *"What are you going to do with it?"*

What was I going to do with the depth and breadth of knowledge, skills, and experience I'd acquired that the world needs and was waiting for?

I'm happy I listened.

I not only made the turn, but now, as my father looks down on me, I know he can clearly see what I'm doing with my talents and gifts.

Creating an online program allows you to:

- Serve more clients.

- Streamline your process.

- Give your clients the ability to connect and learn from others, so they don't ever have to feel alone.

The Career Compass™ has helped me better serve my one-on-one coaching clients, because it perfectly prepares them to take focused action to get what they want. Half the battle of successfully transitioning or advancing in your career is having the right mindset and belief that you *can* actually make it happen. As I always say, *"You can't see beyond your own limitations."* My program helps my clients get past those limitations to get to what they want most.

My advice to you is to use your program to help your clients get past whatever obstacles are holding them back from the results and success they want. Doing so will also open up more time in your schedule, because you're able to support more people at once ... not to mention giving you the ability to offer your services at what may be considered a more affordable price, while still increasing your income.

You can also use it as a stepping-stone to other offers. For example, my program introduces my clients to my Courageously Called Collective™ Mastermind, which is my exclusive high-ticket program for women who want the community, accountability, and on-going support to step into a career of their dreams.

So, are you ready to package your brilliance and present it to the world? I'll leave it to you to answer my father's question …

"What are you going to do with it?"

Dr. Carol Parker Walsh, JD, PhD, is a powerful advocate for women unapologetically living life on their terms and doing the work they were meant to do in the world. She empowers women to take control of their life and career. As an executive coach and personal brand strategist, she serves as a catalyst for transformational growth and professional development. Leveraging an almost 30-year career in law and organizational and academic leadership, and training in applied and social psychology and human development, Carol utilizes a custom methodological approach to career coaching and career development to help her clients achieve greater confidence, clarity, and success. She is a TEDx speaker, two-

time best-selling author, international keynote, and award-winning consultant who has been the "go to" coach for Grammy Award Winners, Paralympic Gold Medalists, Fortune 500 executives, and six- to seven-figure successful, driven professionals and entrepreneurs. You can learn more about her here: carolparkerwalsh.com.

Get Dr. Carol's free gift …

FREE Masterclass: **Unplug From the Career Matrix: 3 Proven Steps to Take Control & Get to the Career You Love!** here:

TeachYourExpertiseBook.com/gifts

ABOUT Alina Vincent

Alina Vincent is a business strategist, speaker, and author. She's also the creator of the Money Making Program Blueprint program and 5-Day Challenge Launch Formula, which are based on the very same strategies she used to grow her business from zero to over a million dollars in just four years.

Alina is passionate about helping entrepreneurs package and monetize their knowledge and expertise to create leveraged and scalable businesses. Experts hire her for strategic advice and simple step-by-step approach to creating successful online programs, engaged Facebook communities, and profitable 5-Day Challenges.

You can learn more about her here: BusinessSuccessEdge.com.

Join her Facebook group here:

facebook.com/groups/BusinessOwnersWhoThinkBig.

BONUS GIFTS

This book comes with free gifts, exercises, and resources from each of the contributing authors.

You can access all of them on the bonus Resources Page:

TeachYourExpertiseBook.com/gifts

Made in USA - North Chelmsford, MA

09.15.2020 1437